Mysterious Phenomena of the Human Psyche

Mysterious
Phenomena
of the
Human Psyche

Leonid L. Vasiliev

Translated by Sonia Volochova

Introduction by Felix Morrow

UNIVERSITY BOOKS *New Hyde Park, New York*

Introduction

SINCE THE DEATH OF STALIN in 1953, there have been many signs that the Soviet leadership, however haltingly, is trying to rejoin the human race. Stalin's megalomania saddled the Soviet mind for decades with ways of thought and feeling more and more alien to civilized humanity of the Twentieth Century. As a result, there is in the Soviet Union a period which is likely to be known in history as *the Stalin gap*: the decades in which the minds of the Soviet population were cut off from Western civilization in myriad ways. The Stalin gap begins with the ascendancy of Stalin over Trotsky in 1923. But this ascendancy does not become total (madness, too, is something that grows) until the early 1930's. Once it becomes total, there is no let-up, it remains until his death in 1953. Then, slowly, it begins to lift. In literature, there begins "the thaw," more evident one year than another, but really continuing. The concentration camps are emptied. The Soviet scientists, academicians, writers, who have been unpersons for ten years, some for twenty years, appear again, worn and prematurely aged, but alive — those who did survive. It takes nearly twelve years, from Stalin's death in 1953 until early 1965, for Stalin's biology, headed by Lysenko, to be finally overthrown.

Here, then, is one such country of the mind: parapsychology. Here is one such scientist, Vasiliev, the author of this book. Professor Vasiliev is now 74 years old; and was graduated from Petersburg University in 1914 as a teacher of the biological sciences: that means he was a thoroughly trained scientist well before the Stalin gap. He was head of the Physiology Department, Bekhterev Brain Institute, Leningrad, 1921-1938.* He appears to have been well acquainted in the 1920's with the work then going on in the field of parapsychology. At that time, too, he appears to have done laboratory and experimental work in parapsychology, in the footsteps of his French masters, especially Charles Richet (1850-1935). How much was he able to follow what went on in the outside world in this field during the Stalin gap? To judge by the two books of his that I have read, this one and his earlier *Mental Suggestion at a Distance,* he was able to read little of anything. How much *work* in parapsychology was he able to do during the Stalin gap? Little, if anything, if one can judge from these books. From 1953 until 1959 he was still silent. In 1959 he published a pamphlet defending the study of parapsychology. In 1962 he published the first edition of the present book, which "touched only lightly on parapsychological findings." In the present, second, edition of the book, Vasiliev says: "I thought it desirable to add two new chapters, which contain information on this branch of psychology worth noting." There is still great caution! "What in this information may eventually be cast out as errors of observation and delusions of the mind, the future will show." By now, Professor Vasiliev has a full-fledged parapsychology laboratory, the first in the Soviet Union, in Leningrad. One hears that other such laboratories have been opened in Moscow, and elsewhere.

Not everything was forbidden during the Stalin gap. Not everything was equally forbidden. It is quite certain, however,

---

*From 1938 (the year of the greatest purge) until 1943 he disappears. Those years are a blank in his biography in *Biographical Dictionary of Parapsychology.* (New York, 1964). In 1943 he reappears again, as Professor of Physiology at Leningrad University until the present time.

that Vasiliev now heads the study of parapsychology in the
Soviet Union. It is almost equally certain that parapsychology
was totally forbidden to him and the Soviet Union, say, from
1930 to 1955.

Now he emerges into the light again and it is not surprising that he does not understand what has been going on mean-
while in the Western world. More surprising, what he does
not understand is not only matters of detail: what literature
has been published, what work has been done during these
twenty-five years. Further, he has no real grasp of the fact that
parapsychology is a pariah in the Western world. He talks of
J. B. Rhine and his Parapsychology Laboratory at Duke University as though there were a Rhine and a parapsychology
laboratory on every substantial university campus in America
and Europe. Vasiliev appears to have not the faintest suspicion
that the laboratory at Duke University is the only one of its
kind in the United States! He does not know that parapsychology is kept alive in the United States only by a handful
of devoted scientists and educated laymen; and that there are
not a dozen campuses (again I limit myself to the United
States, but the European situation is no better) with a single
course in parapsychology. The main institutions that keep
parapsychology alive are outside the academic walls: the American Society for Psychical Research, the Parapsychology Foundation, and a new foundation headed by J. B. Rhine. On the
contrary, Vasiliev really thinks that parapsychology plays a
great role in Western society!

As the Western reader of this book knows very well, parapsychology has so little standing and is so little known, that
my first duty to him is to tell him what parapsychology is! To
begin with, parapsychology is a word of quite recent coinage,
but it is identical in meaning with a term now nearly one
hundred years old: psychical research. In 1859 Darwin shat-
tered (for thinking men) the religious picture of the universe.

But the new science, at least when practiced at its best, made no pretense to solve the riddles of the universe and the destinies of man. There then arose, among some of the very best minds in England, the idea of forming a scientific society to inquire into *psychical* phenomena; it came to fruition when the Society for Psychical Research (SPR) was founded in London in 1882, with the eminent philosopher of Cambridge University, Henry Sidgwick, as the first of its long series of distinguished presidents. It was the purpose of the Society impartially to investigate claims of telepathy and clairvoyance, apparitions and haunted houses; to study hypnotism and so-called mesmeric trance; to inquire into various *physical* phenoma produced by mediums; and to inquire into possible survival of human personality after death. These, then, are the beginnings of parapsychology, and essentially its definition.

A century of study and work in this field has produced a quite substantial literature, even if we limit this literature to the most important items. From a strictly scientific point of view, perhaps the most important part of this literature is the Proceedings of the Society of Psychical Research (England) continuously published since 1882, and the parallel Proceedings published by the American Society for Psychical Research almost as continually since 1890. From the point of view of the educated lay reader, however, more important are the books, usually beginning as material in these Proceedings, but later developed in book form, and which are the veritable landmarks of the development of parapsychology. A short list of the most notable of these books appears at the end of this Introduction.

One such book, G. N. M. Tyrrell's *Science and Psychical Phenomena*, quite typically divides the whole field into two parts. Part I deals with *spontaneous* extrasensory perception. Here are the vivid dreams, coming unbidden and seemingly capriciously, which bring knowledge of events which could not

be known to the dreamer by normal sensory means; the apparitions seen by persons awake and in good health announcing
the death of a distant loved one thought to be alive and well
at the time; the visions or "motor automatisms" which lead to
the discovery of underground water or ore; the hunches so
irresistible that action is taken which saves a life. Part I thus
deals in the main with telepathy, clairvoyance and precognition as they naturally arise in the world.

This leads to Part II, which concerns itself with *experimental* extrasensory perception. Here, a deliberate attempt is
made to elicit paranormal function in the human subject. He
may be asked to identify the suits of playing cards concealed
from his view; or to reproduce drawings being looked at by
"agents" many miles away; or predict the order of a deck of
cards as it will be after thorough shuffling. In Tyrrell's book,
there is a review of the most important work carried out along
this line between 1882 and 1938, with special emphasis on his
own successful experiments with his adopted daughter and
the experiments of J. B. Rhine at Duke University.

Thanks to the Stalin gap, and to the still continuing state
of mind in the Soviet Union, Professor Vasiliev hardly dares
to deal with Part I: *spontaneous* extrasensory perception. That
is, he hardly dares deal with it except parenthetically and in
passing. However, this main division in the two fields of extrasensory perception is the necessary clue to understanding how
he develops the subject (his Chapter I is little more than a
ritualistic assertion of his loyalty to dialectic materialism).
Chapter II deals with sleep and dreams. Why Professor Vasiliev
begins there will be puzzling to a reader who does not know
that this is where Tyrrell and all the masters of parapsychology
begin. Professor Vasiliev devotes Chapter III to hypnotism and
suggestion; here, again, he follows the general outlines of
Western parapsychology, again without explanation. To understand this major chapter, and much of the rest of the book, the

reader needs to know a few salient facts about the history of hypnotism and its relation to psychical research.

Hypnotism is widely accepted today as a legitimate field of scientific inquiry and a useful tool of psychotherapy. But this widespread interest dates only from the Second World War. Previously, hypnosis had a checkered career over a period of centuries, going through cycle after cycle of tentative general approval and then total eclipse. In one of these cycles, at the beginning of the Nineteenth Century, pioneer doctors performed surgery on hypnotised persons, successfully using hypnosis as an anesthetic; but the medical societies insisted that the patients were only pretending not to feel pain and, in effect, outlawed hypnotism. In the 1880's hypnotism was in a period of ascendancy, notably under Charcot and Bernheim in France. But this ascendancy by no means meant general acceptance by either medicine or the educated public. Hence it is that the founders of the Society for Psychical Research in England included hypnotism among its tasks. The hypnotists of that period did a great deal of work of two kinds which obviously belong to parapsychology. One was to hypnotise subjects in order to elicit paranormal phenomena: what Vasiliev calls "far-sight": for example, describing what someone is doing in a laboratory in another city at that moment. The second was to hypnotise patients at a distance. It is an astonishing fact that this work, done under scientific conditions quite impeccably, from about 1880 until the 1920's, was then abandoned quite completely. It is one of the great merits of Vasiliev's work that his *Mental Suggestion at a Distance* may serve to revive this field of work. It is clear from Vasiliev's writings that there is widespread Soviet interest in experiments in which normal consciousness is changed, either by hypnosis or drugs, in order to heighten the extrasensory abilities of the subject. Soviet investigators appear to be especially interested in what is known in the West as "eyeless vision." This Soviet interest has been widely reported in Western newspapers in cases of hypnotised girls reading through their fingertips. In this field Professor Vasiliev seems to give wholehearted acceptance. He appears not to know that there is a considerable literature in the West on this subject, including a notable book by the famous novelist Jules Romains, *Eyeless Sight,* which was, however, the object of considerable criticism by parapsychologists. More than one sensational event of the past was punctured by the discovery of inadequate control of the "eyeless" seer. Skilled magicians learned from this how to put on great vaudeville performances with apparently complete blindfolds through which, or around which, they were able to see. If the numerous Soviet reports in this field remain substantiated it will be a genuine Soviet first in the field of parapsychology.

Professor Vasiliev's next chapter, Chapter IV, dealing with suggestion and autosuggestion, I find especially admirable. Few scientists in the West, even few parapsychologists, are as categorical as he in his acceptance of the reality of the changes made by means of suggestion and autosuggestion. It may be that here he stands on firm ground in the Soviet Union; that Soviet psychiatry is devoted in large part, so far as therapy is concerned, to the direct use of suggestion either by hypnotism or in the waking state.

Beyond Chapter IV, the Western reader needs no further guidelines. From this point on Professor Vasiliev is, quite openly, a proponent of parapsychology. It is true that he prefers to call telepathy "brain broadcasting." He is more comfortable in being able to point to one of the undoubted great frontiers of scientific study: the electrical currents generated in all parts of the human body and mind. He reports, quite seriously, that Soviet scientists have invented a mechanical hand for amputees which is moved, not by the remaining muscles, but by electrical brain currents which put the fingers of the mechanical hand into motion even when the operator merely thinks of the movement. I find this report quite astounding and, quite frankly, I shall not believe it until it is duplicated by Western scientists.

I call the reader's attention especially to Chapter VIII: Is Transmission of Muscular Power at a Distance Possible? Vasiliev says: "In the near future we may expect to utilize at a distance instrumentally amplified radio waves originating from the muscles, heart, and brain in behalf of practical needs of one kind or another." These radio waves will be received by natural receivers, animals and humans, and also by man-made receivers: computers. Vasiliev does not go into this, but his work, in turn, is one of the forerunners of the new field of bio-cybernetics, which is being pursued both in the West and in the Soviet Union. The reader not previously exposed to such ideas may blink in bewilderment but it is nevertheless a fact that serious scientists in both worlds are trying to find ways and means to direct computers by mental suggestion. I hope to present a volume of papers in bio-cybernetics in the near future. It is not an easy field in which to collect material. Both in the West and in the Soviet Union, most of this material is still classified as secret, for both sides are trying to find ways and means of weaponizing bio-cybernetics. The term weaponizing may sound barbaric but it is an important term today in conferences of scientists convened by the Central Intelligence Agency of the United States.

The founders of parapsychology were scientists or educated laymen who accepted scientific canons of evidence as the limits within which parapsychology should be pursued. Their interest in parapsychology, however, was not science. Human needs no longer satisfied by religion led them to parapsychology. In England, the story of parapsychology begins on a night in the year 1869 in Cambridge, when F. W. H. Myers and Henry Sidgwick met to take a starlight walk. Here were two brilliant scholars, no longer able to believe in Christianity. Myers later wrote of this meeting: "I felt drawn in my perplexities to Henry Sidgwick as somehow my only hope...I asked him, almost with trembling, whether he thought that when Tradition, Intuition, Metaphysics has failed to solve the riddle of the Universe, there was still a chance that for many actual observable phenomena — ghosts, spirits, whatsoever there might be — some valid knowledge might be drawn as to a World Unseen." Professor Sidgwick told Myers that this empirical approach to the riddles of the universe and the destinies of man had long been in his mind.

Now, after the Stalin gap, these same human needs are able to emerge in the Soviet Union; hence Professor Vasiliev's work in parapsychology, and its official encouragement by the Soviet Government. It is true that one can make out a case for the idea that the Soviet Government is seeking ways and means of weaponizing parapsychology. In this and his other books Professor Vasiliev makes as much as he can of the report, which appeared in 1959, that the United States Navy was conducting telepathic experiments between a land installation and the submerged submarine *Nautilus*. The story has been discredited by the United States Government and we in the West, who know how little standing parapsychology has, including research in telepathy, can take for this the word of our government. Given Vasiliev's mistaken notion of the reigning power of parapsychology in the West, one can understand his naive belief in the story. One can also make out a case for the notion that each side is escalating the other in the field of parapsychology, thanks to fear of the other. Frightened or at least fascinated by the Nautilus story, the Soviet Government gave its blessing and a laboratory to Professor Vasiliev's old love. No government money and very little foundation money has ever been given for parapsychological research in the United States. But the other day, the government-financed

National Institute of Mental Health gave a grant to a New
York professor of psychology to pursue experiments in eyeless
sight: the professor is quite patently imitating the work
reported by Vasiliev, has never previously been associated in
any way with parapsychology and, I suspect, does not know
the literature. But if there is escalation of parapsychology on
both sides, it is all to the good, and we can be fairly certain
(those of us who really know something about the century of
parapsychology) that neither side will find a way to
weaponize it.

Far more important is the significance of this emergence
of parapsychology in the Soviet Union as a sign of renewed
recognition of spiritual needs. When you open the door to the
study of telepathy, precognition, extrasensory perception, the
hidden powers of the mind, you open the door to the evidence
of things not seen and never likely to be seen. It means that
many riddles of the universe will remain riddles. It means that
human destiny is wrapped in eternal mystery. It means to
sense the narrow limits of science and its limited place in the
life of humanity. It leads away from power and pelf and
toward meditation and moderation. It is a sign, too, of the re-
emergence of the Russian soul, of Tolstoy and Dostoievsky, of
Russian music and art, and the mystical traditions of the Eastern
Orthodox Church. "Man's heart is a dark forest," says the old
Russian proverb. It is true, in a quite unique way, about the
Russian people. Western Europe has recognized and respected
for a long time this unique aspect of Russia, in its best expressions in literature, art and religion. Professor Vasiliev's work
in parapsychology is an oblique, but nonetheless significant sign,
that after the long Stalin gap the Soviet peoples are being per-
mitted to rejoin the human race.

FELIX MORROW

SELECTED BOOKS
ON PARAPSYCHOLOGY IN ENGLISH

BESTERMAN, THEODORE. Crystal Gazing. intro. by Eve Juster. xxxii + 183 pp. bibliog. index. $5.00

BERNHEIM, H. Hypnosis and Suggestion in Psychotherapy: The Nature and Use of Hypnotism. intro. by Ernest R. Hilgard. index. 428 pp. 6⅛" x 9¼" 63-22664. $10.00

BIRREN, FABER. Color: A Survey in Words and Pictures: From Ancient Mysticism to Modern Science. ill. index. 250 pp. 7⅝" x 10½" 62-18889. $15.00

FEILDING, EVERARD. Sittings with Eusapia Palladino and other Studies. intro. by E. J. Dingwall. 324 pp. 6⅛" x 9¼" 63-18682. $10.00

FLOURNOY, THEODORE. From India to the Planet Mars. intro. and final chap. by C. T. K. Chari. xxxvi + 469 pp. 5½" x 8½" 63-16228. $10.00

Fox, OLIVER. Astral Projection: A Record of Out-of-the-Body Experiences. fwd. by John C. Wilson. xiii + 160 pp. 5½" x 8½" 62-19195. $5.00

JAFFE, ANIELA. Apparitions and Precognitions: A Study from the Point of View of C. G. Jung's Analytical Psychology. intro. by C. G. Jung. index. 224 pp. 6⅛" x 9¼" 63-19744. $7.50

JAMES, WILLIAM. The Varieties of Religious Experience: A Study in Human Nature. Enlarged Edition with Appendixes and Introduction by Joseph Ratner. index. bibliog. 672 pp. 6⅛" x 9¼" 63-14505. $10.00

MYERS, F. W. H. Human Personality and its Survival of Bodily Death. ed. by Susy Smith, fwd. by Aldous Huxley. index. 416 pp. 6¼" x 9¼" 61-9319. $10.00

OSBORN, ARTHUR W. The Future is Now: The Significance of Precognition. intro. by Eileen J. Garrett. index. 254 pp. 6⅛" x 9¼" 61-9321. $6.00

PODMORE, FRANK. Mediums of the 19th Century. intro. by Eric J. Dingwall. index. xxvii + 720 pp. 2 volumes bound in buckram and slipcased. 6⅛" x 9¼" 63-10384. $20.00

PODMORE, FRANK. From Mesmer to Christian Science: A Short History of Mental Healing. intro. by E. J. Dingwall. index. xxi + 306 pp. 6⅛" x 9¼" 63-21599. $10.00

PRINCE, WALTER FRANKLIN. The Case of Patience Worth. intro. by John C. Wilson. 509 pp. 6⅛" x 9¼" 63-23268. $10.00

SIDGWICK, ELEANOR MILDRED. Phantasms of the Living: Cases of Telepathy Printed in the Journal of the Society for Psychical Research During Thirty-Five Years; and Phantasms of the Living, by Edmund Gurney, Frederic W. H. Myers & Frank Podmore; abridged & ed. by Eleanor Mildred Sidgwick. xxxvi + 462 + 520 pp. 6⅛" x 9¼" 62-17319. $15.00

SMITH, SUSY. The Mediumship of Mrs. Leonard. photographs. bibliog. 256 pp. 6⅛" x 9¼" 64-17317. $7.50

SPENCE, LEWIS. An Encyclopedia of Occultism: a Compendium of Information on the Occult Science, Occult Personalities, Psychic Science, Magic, Demonology, Spiritism, Mysticism and Metaphysics. ill. b/w 244 plates. bibliog. index. xxiv + 440 pp. 8" x 10" 59-15875. $15.00

All these books are published by University Books, Inc., New Hyde Park, New York 11041.

PUBLISHER'S NOTE

In the Russian edition, the author's book is printed on newsprint, and contains forty line illustrations. Thanks to the poor method of reproduction, most of them cannot be reproduced. These include:

1. Siamese twins
2. A yoga asleep (autohypnosis)
3. Sleepwalker
4. Hypnotism as practiced in Greek temples
5. Chicken hypnotized
6. Mesmer magnetizing women patients
7. Hypnotist at work
8. Sleep induced by verbal suggestion
9. Hypnotic passes administered with the aid of an electric heater
10. Verbal inducement of sleep
11. Professor Mangold's machine for hypnotizing animals
12. Mother applying verbal suggestion to child during night sleep
13. Hypnotic in a state of lethargy
14. Plastic tone of muscles of hypnotics
15. Mark left by a burst blister caused by suggestion of a burn instilled during hypnotic sleep
16. Mass hypnosis by the celebrated stage hypnotist N. A. Smirnov
17. Loss of sensitivity to pain in a hypnotized woman

18. Loss of sensitivity to pain in a hypnotized chicken
19. Tibetan lama with prayer drum
20. Spiritualist séance
21. Ideomotor act — induced swinging and rotation of pendulum

As will be seen from these examples, most of the illustrations are borrowed from books by Vasiliev's French masters. Illustrations referring to recent Soviet work will be found at the end of this book.

Contents

INTRODUCTION BY FELIX MORROW   V

I.   Mysterious Phenomena of the Human Psyche
     as the Source of Superstitions   3

II. Sleep and Dreams   11

III. Hypnotism and Suggestion   37

IV. Suggestion and Autosuggestion During
     the Waking State   83

V.   Automatic Movements   101

VI. Does "Brain Broadcasting" Exist?   119

VII. What Can Be Said about "Extrasensory
     Perception?"   149

VIII. Is Transmission of Muscular Power
      at a Distance Possible?   169

IX. Death and the Superstitions
     Associated with It   187

     Illustrations   207

     Index   213

Mysterious Phenomena of the Human Psyche as the Source of Superstitions

CHAPTER I

Mysterious Phenomena of the Human Psyche as the Source of Superstitions

SUPERSTITIONS AND PREJUDICES were engendered in the remote past, when the study of nature and man was in its infancy, and every unusual phenomenon was an enigma and a mystery. Man, confronted by a nature full of secrets and marvels, seemed helpless. Eclipses of the sun and moon, comets, meteors, tempests — all terrifying cosmic and meteorological phenomena — were interpreted as auguries of wars, famine, the plague, and other national calamities.

In a class society general fears are intensified by the worker's peonage to the ruling masters, in whose hands he is a mere plaything and his life a pawn which may, at any moment, be risked on the throw of a card to satisfy the greed of feudal conquerors or exploiting capitalists. Thus, ignorance of the laws governing the development of human society consolidates man's fear of incomprehensible phenomena of nature and transforms superstitions into a means for the spiritual enslavement of the masses.

Terrifying and incomprehensible biological phenomena also engender superstitions. Epidemics of smallpox, cholera, the plague, and other catastrophic diseases, which in ancient times decimated entire nations, were thought to be punishment from a wrathful god, machinations of the devil, or spells cast by sorcerers and witches. Mental disorders, which at times developed into "psychic epidemics," were interpreted as possession by a malevolent spirit, madness, the plague, the "evil eye," or as the consequence of dabbling with magic. In the Middle Ages approximately nine million people accused of commerce with the devil perished at the stake or died by torture. The last burning of a sorcerer at the stake by the Spanish Inquisition took place in 1780.

Vestiges of these once formidable superstitions were preserved in our own country up to the very eve of the great Socialist October Revolution, in the form of hysteria, conjuring, fortune-telling, faith in omens and amulets, belief in predestination (whatever is is preordained"), and the like.

Occasional reports of some rare instances of popular superstition of one kind or another appear in our press even today. Only recently it was reported that in the city of Orsk a certain Tamara Petrovna, masquerading as a "sorceress," "cured" young girls of the "plague" by quackery, extorting money and clothes from them.[1] A similar instance, known to me personally, occurred in so cultural a center as Leningrad.

Let me cite another case of blind faith verging on insane fanaticism. A mother of two, whose husband had left her, hoped, "with God's help," to bring him back by crawling

---

[1] *Komsomolskaya pravda*, December 24, 1958.

around a "holy" lake on her knees. When she was brought to a hospital, she was barely able to stand on her feet and her knees were bruised and bloody.[2]

Marxist-Leninist philosophy has shown us that superstitions and prejudices are not engendered only by lack of knowledge of the true laws of nature, not only by the ignorance and poverty of the masses which capitalist exploitation fosters. The anarchy which is inherent in capitalist production generates in man, all by itself, a feeling of helplessness before the forces of social development that are alien to him, and it is this feeling which predisposes him to a mystical view of reality.

The greatness of the scientific achievement of Karl Marx and Friedrich Engels, rests, in part, on the fact that by revealing the true laws of social development they created the prerequisites for the liquidation of religio-mystical prejudices.

The Soviet Union has declared relentless war on superstition. Our whole social structure, with its systematic day-by-day dissemination of political and scientific knowledge among the masses, is directed at the total extirpation of pseudo-scientific doctrines concerning nature, man, and society. The sources of a great many of our superstitions and prejudices have already dried up: what Soviet citizen would still attribute a mystical significance to such phenomena as, for instance, an eclipse of the sun, or a flu epidemic?

One area of the ideological battlefront, however, requires special attention — superstitions engendered by inadequate and naive comprehension of certain actual neuropsychic phenomena.

---

[2] *Zvezda*, No. 12, 1958.

These phenomena pertain primarily to the realm of twilight states of consciousness and to the various motor automatisms. Some of them are highly commonplace, or encountered quite frequently; for instance, dreams, various manifestations of suggestion and autosuggestion in the waking state. Others are, on the contrary, rare, but exert, for this very reason, a more powerful effect on the imagination. This category includes hallucinations, various aspects of hypnotic sleep, and other psychopathological phenomena found mainly in persons suffering from more or less advanced hysteria.

At the present time a new scientific theory, called parapsychology, or metapsychology,[3] is being quite widely disseminated abroad. It has set for itself the task of either corroborating or definitely refuting, by observation and specially devised experiments, the existence of certain rarely encountered and seemingly incredible psychic, or even rather, psychophysiological, phenomena. These phenomena include: perception of some other person's psychic experiences without their transmission by means of speech or any other sense organ (so-called direct transmission of thoughts or emotions, in other words — telepathy); perception of objects and events without the mediation of any sensory organ known to us (extrasensory perception,[4] telesthesia, old-fashioned clairvoyance); transmission at a distance of muscular energy and of its mechanical power over

---

[3] The Greek prefixes "para" (near) and "meta" (after) emphasize the fact that parapsychic (metapsychic) phenomena fall outside traditional psychology's field of observation. In abbreviated form these "paranormal" psychic phenomena are indicated by the Greek letter "psi" — ψ.
[4] Abbreviated as ESP.

both animate and inanimate objects (so-called telekinesis).[5]

Despite the fact that paraphychological phenomena do not accord well with what at this time is considered as generally recognized in science, materialists should neither ignore nor reject *a priori* everything related to such phenomena. For if we reject patient experimental checking of these phenomena, we rearm the idealists, and thereby aid and abet them in deepening the roots of superstition.[6]

However, the most important, most universal source of popular superstition and religious belief has always been, and still is, the mentally disturbing phenomenon of death. The fear of death and anguished grief at the loss of people near and dear gave rise to one of religion's main bulwarks —belief in the immortality of the soul, or in its subsequent reincarnation

---

[5] One must give credit to the French scientists investigating these phenomena. However incredible the facts appear to be, they do not deviate from a true scientific approach. This is as true of Charles Richet, who published, in 1921, the first compilation of parapsychological data (Ch. Richet, *Traité de métapsychique*, Paris, 1921), as it is of his successors — Eugène Osty, J. Roux, R. Warcollier, R. Kherumian, and the latest French compilation of parapsychological data by Robert Amadou (*La Parapsychologie: Essai historique et critique*, Paris, 1954). Regretfully, the same cannot be said of many English and American parapsychologists, who frequently admix their parapsychological investigations with their idealistic philosophical convictions and religious beliefs. These sins were first committed by the Anglo-American founders of parapsychology — William Barrett, F. W. H. Myers, William Crookes, William James.

[6] In the first edition of *Mysterious Phenomena of the Human Psyche*, in the chapter entitled "Does a Brain Radio exist?", I touched only lightly on parapsychological findings. In the present, second, edition of the book, I thought it desirable to add two new chapters, which contain information on this branch of psychology worth noting. What in this information may eventually be cast out as errors of observation and delusions of the mind, the future will show.

among the living; or, at least, in the transient existence of some posthumous remnant of the self, able to communicate with the living.

In pre-revolutionary times, the phenomena we have enumerated were an inexhaustible source of religious and popular beliefs, omens, readings, and magical methods of doctoring and of fortune-telling. Among the more educated classes the same phenomena begot various occult (secret) "theories" with scientific pretensions: for instance, animal magnetism, mediumism, spiritualism, and so on. It must be confessed that vestiges of this heritage from the past are still with us.

The struggle against popular and "scientific" superstition cannot, and must not, be waged apart from anti-religious propaganda. So long as religion exists, so long will superstitious notions, incompatible with the attainments of science, remain secreted in the minds of some men and, from time to time, spring to life again.

Our task is to remove the aura of mystery from phenomena that give rise to superstition: to explain them scientifically. The great discoveries of I. M. Sechenov and I. P. Pavlov in the field of physiology of the brain and of higher nervous activity and, especially, Pavlov's theory of sleep and dreams, hypnosis and suggestion — supplemented by the findings of materialistic psychology and psychopathology — furnish excellent weapons in our combat with superstition. One of the newest branches of medical science — thanatology, the study of the processes of death and the possible resuscitation of living creatures, including man — also serves as such a weapon.

CHAPTER II

Sleep
and Dreams

CHAPTER II

Sleep
and Dreams

IN ANCIENT TIMES dreams were assumed to be divine revelations. People believed that good and evil spirits could enter man's sleeping body and through dreams communicate to him diverse information, influence him to commit some deed, or predict events for him. However, it was noted even then that in dreams both gods and spirits preferred to appear in vague, at times symbolic, form, leaving the unraveling of their secret meaning to man himself. This was considered a difficult task, which only priests and professional interpreters of dreams could undertake.

This view of dreams was related to animism (from the Latin *anima* — soul). It was thought that during sleep the soul could temporarily separate from the body and transpose itself into the past or future, while still retaining some tie with the body. It was further believed that during its wanderings the soul acquired various impressions which were perceived by the sleeper in the form of dreams — images of never-seen lands, of mysterious objects, or of known or unknown persons, living or dead.

In time, these notions were complemented by other more elaborate, but similarly naive conceptions: the soul does not leave the body during sleep; instead, psychic powers, hidden when man is awake, awaken when he is asleep, among them the most important — clairvoyance: the power to foresee the future and to learn of events occurring at a remote distance. Both are perceived by the sleeper in some mysterious way, without the participation of his sensory organs, and are experienced as dreams.

These notions produced, as far back as antiquity, a special type of reading by dreams — "oneiromancy." In the second century B.C. a certain Artemidorus, a Greek from Daldis, circulated the first "dream book." The following excerpt from his book exemplifies this art of dream interpretation: "If an artisan sees that he has many hands, it is a good omen: he will always have plenty of work. The dream signifies that he will need many hands. In addition, it augurs well for those who are diligent and lead an orderly life. I have often observed that it designates more children and slaves, and greater wealth. For swindlers, however, the dream, by betokening that many hands will be occupied with him, presages jail."

In the Middle Ages even philosophers and physicians became dream interpreters. The most authoritative of these was the physician Kardanus (sixteenth century). His interpretations were carefully transcribed by subsequent compilers of "dream books" up to the twentieth century. Comparing the miscellany of "dream books," we see that the same dream was at various times interpreted differently.

There also existed popular omens related to dreams. And

while the majority of them are the purest nonsense, it cannot be denied that some contain a modicum of folk wisdom and keen observation. The noted Russian physiologist, N. E. Vvedensky, who perceived the hidden sense of some popular omens, had this to say on the subject:

"What is remarkable is the fact that the deeper the sleep, the greater is the number of associations from early life and the larger the number of interpretations that it evokes, as if light sleep affects only the more superficial layer of memory, whereas deep sleep evokes interpretations from the realm of much deeper, long-discarded, recordings. Our peasants believe that a dream of long-dead parents presages bad weather; nor does this lack sense, for impending bad weather induces deep somnolence, which is characterized by the appearance of images from the distance past."[1]

The scientific approach to the study of dreams was initiated at the end of the eighteenth century. One of the first more or less serious works on this question, Dr. Nudov's *A Tentative Formulation of a Theory of Sleep,*[2] appeared in 1791. The author, by the way, cites a valuable observation, which has served as the point of departure for subsequent researchers in the same field. A few drops of water were poured into the open mouth of a man who was sleeping on his back; the sleeper turned on his stomach and began to make swimming motions with his hands and feet; he dreamt that he had fallen into water and had to save himself by swimming.

---

[1] N. E. Vvedensky, *Polnoye sobranie sochineniy* (Collected Works), Leningrad, 1954, V, p. 337.
[2] *Opyt postroyenia teorii sna.*

Such observations show that dreams may be induced by some accidental stimulation of one or another sense organ. More than that, by subjecting the sleeper to such a stimulus — sound, light, touch — it is possible, on occasion, to induce, intentionally, dreams which clearly correspond to the character of the applied stimulus. Thus the way was opened for the experimental study of dreams. The French scholar, Mori, and the German scholar, Weygandt, who devoted their lives to inquiries into the causes of dreams, worked especially hard in this field. In Russia the problem was studied by V. M. Bekhterev and M. I. Astvatsaturov; the latter studied the features of dream content in people with various ailing organs, and was one of the first to utilize dreams for diagnosing illness.

Mori relates that once, while he was asleep, a bottle of *eau de cologne* was applied to his nose; the whiff was enough to provoke in him, instantaneously, a dream of a perfume shop, Cairo, and oriental lands that he had recently visited. In another experiment Mori directed a red light into the face of a sleeping person; the experimental subject dreamt of a storm, flashes of lightning, thunderbolts. In a Swiss hotel crowded with travelers, nearly all the guests dreamt, one stormy night, the same dream; that with a deafening din carriages filled with new travelers were driving into the courtyard, crowding the guests still more. These facts attest to the influence of external stimuli on the activity of the brain during sleep.

Another fact common to dreams is equally interesting: dreams rich in content, which seem to the dreamer to last a long time, actually flow by very quickly — within a few seconds. In dreams, conceptions of time and space are sharply distorted, as instanced by the following example. A well-known play-wright fell asleep, from fatigue and illness, during a performance of his play. Dreaming, he saw the entire play, from beginning to end, followed its progress, and watched the audience's reaction. At last the curtain was lowered, the dramatist woke up, and discovered, to his amazement, that on the stage the play had not progressed beyond the opening remarks of the first scene. Thus, in his dream, the entire performance of the play had occupied but a few seconds.[3]

That events and memories may at times pass through the mind with extraordinary and supernormal speed during the waking state as well is attested by the depositions of men who have lived through a moment of mortal danger. It is claimed that at such a moment memories of practically one's whole life obtrude into the mind.

No less frequent a source of dreams are the excitations aroused not by the external world but by the internal organs of the body — stomach, intestines, urinary bladder, lungs, heart, and others. All these organs are sensitive and connected by means of nervous pathways to the "psychic organ" — the cerebral cortex. During the day we do not as a rule notice

---

[3] Until recently, similar instances of the speed-up of psychic activity during sleep were not questioned. Lately, however, researches conducted by American psychologists at the University of Chicago established that during the period of the sleeper's dreaming his brain waves resemble those present during waking states, and that under the lowered eyelids the eyeballs are intensely active. As a rule this activity lasts as long as the dream, an average of nine minutes; occasionally, however, it may last much longer. It was found that "the activity observed by the sleeper in a dream consumes exactly as much time as it would have consumed had it taken place during the waking state." (See the journal *Tekhnika-molodezhi*, No. 9 [1962], p. 33.)

the "signals" that emanate from the internal organs, because our conscious mind is filled with the more powerful impressions of the external world. At night the situation changes: the less active the external sense organs, the more acute is our awareness of the stimuli emanating from the internal organs, especially if these stimuli are aroused by some pathological processes. This engenders the distressing nightmarish dreams that frighten superstitious people. The disruption of the normal functioning of the heart or respiration during sleep is the most frequent source of such dreams. When this occurs, we dream that, exhausted from fatigue and pursued by wild beasts or robbers, we keep on running, or that we are in danger of drowning, or are suffocating in fire and flames. During his experiments the German psychologist, Berner, used to close up the sleeper's nose with cotton, and invariably observed the following results: the sleeper would begin to toss about and moan. When he awoke, he would relate a nightmare wherein a monster, who grew progressively larger, threatened to smother him. "The house brownie[4] was choking you!" the peasants would declare in the old days when the conversation turned to such dreams.

Dreams aroused by stimulation of the internal organs may have diagnostic significance. An experienced physician might discern in them the incipient stages of some internal illness that had not as yet shown its characteristic symptoms during the patient's waking state. There are many examples of this. One patient dreamt that one of his legs had "turned to stone" and could no longer function: shortly afterward the leg became

---

[4] *Domovoy.*

paralyzed. Another patient had for several months been dreaming that he was swallowing various objects: the reason for this oft-repeated dream was an incipient malignant tumor of the throat. The German naturalist and physician, K. Gesner, dreamt that he had been bitten in the chest by a snake; sometime later an ulcer, which took a long time to heal, appeared in the same place. In all these cases the commencement of the illness eluded the waking mind preoccupied with the routine sensations and cares of the day.

For a long time there was no explanation for the observed influence the activity of the internal organs exerted on the content of dreams. It was the Russian physiologist, I. P. Pavlov, together with his collaborators, and especially K. M. Bykov, who finally exposed the mechanism of the interaction existing between the cerebral cortex and the internal organs. Their work provided the first scientific explanation of the facts described above, and the experiments which they conducted and their observations, establishing the role played by the external and internal organs in the genesis of dreams, paved the way for the contemporary physiological conceptions of the nature of dreams and sleep. Another major discovery was no less significant. In the sixties and seventies of the nineteenth century, it was learned that the psychic functions are localized in the cerebral cortex. It was established that all the sense organs are represented in the cerebral cortex; the visual organ is connected with the occipital area of the brain, the auditory organ with the temporal area, the tactile organ with the parietal area. Shortly afterward, the Russian physician, B. Oks, published a pamphlet that was remarkable for its time. In it, he was already considering dreams as the result of the partial activity of disparate sectors of the brain during sleep. Following is a brief excerpt from this unjustly forgotten work:

"It is easy to imagine that, under the influence of a soporific substance, a given group of cells [the neurons of the cerebral cortex] responsible for some special mental activity, may temporarily cease to function; at the same time the groups still awake continue to function as usual. This partial activity of the brain explains both its minimal mental activity [during sleep] and the incoherence and absurdity of many dreams. Sudden stimulation [of the sense organs] summon anew some region [of the cerebral cortex] to activity; in return, all, or some of the [previously] functioning areas of cells become dormant."[5]

Dreams reflect the partial activity of the cerebral cortex, through inhibition brought on by varied stimulation of the external or internal sensory organs. This is the meaning of the postulates of Dr. Oks quoted above. Formulated eighty years ago, they already approximated the modern theory of sleep and dreams experimentally substantiated by Pavlov and his collaborators. Oks was mistaken only in his conception of what causes inhibition of the brain cells during sleep. He assumed (as did nearly all of his contemporaries) that dreams were a result of the metabolic autointoxication of the brain cells — "the poisons of sleep," which, accumulating in the blood and the cells during the waking states, like narcotics, induce slumber. In reality, we fall asleep before the poisons

---

[5] B. Oks, *Fizioligia sna i snovideniy* (The Physiology of Sleep and Dreams), Odessa, 1880, p. 78.

of metabolism have had a chance to accumulate. It is possible to take a nap even in the morning, after a sufficiently long night's sleep, when there can be no question of the "poisons of sleep." Only in exceptional cases when, sustained by artificial means, one has stayed awake for several days in a row, and the need for sleep has become painful and no longer resistible, does the autointoxication factor begin to play a primary role.

This fact is attested by the interesting experiments carried out in 1939 by Professor P. K. Anokhin of Moscow on a rare subject — Siamese twins. The twins had a common body, a common heart, and a common blood stream, but two heads and two brains. Frequently one head would fall asleep while the other remained awake, a fact indicating that the humoral factor (the composition of the blood) does not play the principal role in inducing sleep: for in the case of the Siamese twins the two brains, though receiving blood of the same composition, were able to function on two different planes, one brain in a state of inhibition, the other in a waking state.

What beneficent factor, then, impels us to fall asleep on schedule, thus protecting our brain and our entire organism against overfatigue or the dangers of autointoxication? In a series of classic experiments utilizing conditioned-reflex methodology, Pavlov demonstrated that inhibition of the nerve cells which compose the cerebral cortex is the factor responsible for inducing sleep.

Rhythmic nervous impulses that flow from the sense organs to the neural cells of the cortex may, under various conditions, have one of two effects on them: either bringing them to an active, excited state or, conversely, inhibiting this

active state, excluding the nerve cells from functioning. Excitation and inhibition are the basic nervous processes. Without
them no motor act, no psychic experience, can be realized.

Excitation and inhibition are thus the two factors, the
two processes, responsible for the realization of higher nervous
activity. Owing to the interaction of these two processes in
the cortex, the analysis and synthesis of external stimulation
take place in correspondence with its importance for the living
activity of the organism; during this interaction the dynamics
of excitation determine also the character of the organism's
response to the influences of its external and internal environment.

The so-called dynamic (labile) "mosaic" of loci of excitation and inhibition in the cerebral cortex corresponds to the
waking state. The spatial distribution between these loci is
constantly shifting in accordance with the activity of the given
moment, or the experienced psychic state. When I am lecturing, the loci of steady excitation are to be found in those
regions of the cortex which control speech functions and bring
about thought; all the other areas of the cortex are in a state
of more or less deep inhibition. But when I shift to another
kind of activity, commence to play the piano for instance, the
"mosaic" of the cortex instantly changes: the previous loci of
excitation are inhibited and new ones are activated in other
groupings of cortical cells. The human cortex contains 14 or
15 billion nerve cells (neurons). The number of possible
spatial combinations of excited and inhibited loci in the cortex
is, indeed, beyond calculation. And each of these combinations
reflects any of several components of various psychic states.

What, then, happens to this cerebral "mosaic" of our waking state when we fall asleep? An especially steady locus of inhibition arises in some cortical area. Weak, monotonous stimuli — a lullaby, rocking, the ticking of a clock, and so on — may help to form such a locus. From this locus inhibition begins to "irradiate" — to spread first to adjacent groups of neurons — then, expanding farther and farther, it extinguishes the loci of excitation it encounters on the way, until it finally takes over the entire cortex, all the cortical neurons. Deep, dreamless sleep ensues. The cerebral cortex — the "psychic organ" — is completely at rest.

It follows that sleep is the result of the predominance of the inhibitory process in the cerebral cortex. This inhibition, as I. P. Pavlov pointed out, has a "protective" significance for the organism, helping it to rest as a whole, and especially its most delicately organized apparatus, the cerebral cortex.

One may therefore say that this process of sleep-inducing inhibition, as it spreads throughout the cortex, plays the role of "guardian angel" to both the brain and the entire organism. More: it sometimes plays the role of "miraculous healer," accelerating in the cerebral cells the reconstitution (resynthesis) of the exceedingly complex chemical compounds, so indispensable to the normal functioning of the brain and the psyche, which are dissipated during daily strenuous activity. Insufficient daily restoration of these compounds causes not only the brain, but also the bodily organs it superintends, to sicken. It is therefore understandable why such illnesses are cured by artificially prolonged sleep, the so-called sleep-therapy, introduced into medical practice by I. P. Pavlov and his followers. There are times, however, when some disturbing thought or creative idea or turbulent emotion keeps us from falling asleep. At such times, loci of unusually intense and steady excitation operate in the cerebral cortex; it is just these which impede the irradiation of inhibition, the coming of sleep. If sleep does come, it is incomplete, partial. Like a solitary rock in a spreading sea of inhibition, some watchdog "outpost of excitation" in the cortex is maintained, enabling the sleeping brain to retain contact with its environment. Thus, exhausted by arduous campaigns, it sleeps, but at the faintest alarm is on its feet again ready to take arms.

In a series of remarkable experiments on dogs, Pavlov and his collaborators (B. N. Birman[6] and others) reproduced similar phenomena. For instance, a conditioned salivary reflex in response to a definite tone on a harmonium — "do" — is formed in a dog. The sounding of this tone is invariably accompanied by an unconditioned salivary stimulus — feeding. Once the conditioned reflex in response to the sound "do" is established, the other tones of the harmonium — "re," "mi," "fa," "sol" — when first sounded also evoke salivation. Since, however, the action of these tones is not reinforced by feeding, salivation is extinguished. Now only the tone "do," which is reinforced by feeding, arouses excitation in the corresponding cortical center. All the other sounds of the harmonium create in the cortex loci of "internal," "differentiating" (to use Pavlov's terminology) inhibition. With only the prolonged sound of one of these inhibitory tones now, "mi," for instance, internal inhibition will begin to irradiate from its locus. When irradiation spreads throughout the cerebral cortex, the dog will fall asleep. Such experimentally induced sleep is in all respects similar to the usual sleep with a "sentinel area" maintained in the cortex; the instant the exciting conditioned stimulus, which has been reinforced by feeding — the tone "do" — is sounded, the dog will awake, start to look for food, and saliva will begin to flow.

Sleep accompanied by dreams is another variety of incomplete inhibition of the cortex. If the sleep is deep, the cortex is deeply inhibited, and excitatory impulses arriving into it from the sense organs are abated. There will be no dreams. Toward morning, when the cortical cells have had sufficient rest, protective inhibition weakens and the impulses that penetrate to the cortex begins to make their way through a labyrinth of neurons dentritically interwoven. Like will-o'-the-wisps, excitation runs from one group of cortical cells to another and by disinhibiting them brings to life a capricious train of predominantly visual images which we call dreams. The vividness and vitality of the images which arise with this are striking. Awake, one's imagination can paint nothing comparable. It is precisely the vividness of the dream images that, evidently, played so important a role in engendering superstitions concerning life after death.

Many features of dreams, and especially their extraordinary and fantastic imagery, are explained by Pavlov's theory of the two signal systems. During the formation of conditioned reflexes the usual external stimuli — sound, light, smell, and so on — become signals of unconditioned stimuli

---

[6] See B. N. Birman, *Experimentalniy son* (Experimental Sleep), Leningrad: Gosizdat, 1925.

and may replace the latter. Thus, for instance, the tone "do" in the above-cited Birman experiment becomes the signal for an alimentary reaction, replacing the unconditioned alimentary stimulus. The combination of such signals and the conditioned reflexes they evoke — the first signal system — forms the basis of the psychic activity of the more highly developed animals, as well as of children who have not yet learned to talk. It predominated in primordial man for whom oral and internal speech (which is directly connected with thinking) were still on a low level of development. Where there is no speech, there are no concepts, no logical thinking (operation with concepts); at these stages of development thinking is possible only by means of concrete images and associations (connections) in accordance with contiguity, similarity, or contrast. But how vivid are these images, how untrammeled and fantastic the associations! With the development of speech a second signal system appeared alongside the first. The word became the auditory symbol of the first system's signals, the "signal of signals;" thinking grew ever more logical, more abstract, losing in the process its primordial imagery; and the higher the verbal system of signals ascends in its evolutionary process (develop-ment), the more is the first signal system (phylogenetically less recent) suppressed, inhibited, put into second place.

What then happens during sleep? Because it is phylo-genetically more recent, the second signal system is less stable and, with the advent of sleep, the first to become inhibited. Thanks to this, the first signal system easily frees itself from its influence; at the same time thinking in images, with its vivid and untrammeled fantasies, acquires an independent meaning. The most improbable, most unreal, dreams are accepted by the sleeper as fact, as truly existing; only when we awake, do we begin to marvel at our credulity during sleep.

During sleep the images of reality are frequently drastically altered, even distorted. This is explained by the existence, discovered by Pavlov's collaborators, of so-called hypnotic phases. These phases appear during transition from waking to sleep and from sleep to waking. Especially significant is the "paradoxical" phase, which is remarkable for the fact that throughout its duration weak external and internal stimuli exert a noticeably greater influence on the brain, and consequently on the psyche, than more intense stimuli. Similarly, traces left by weak impressions in the cerebral cortex are, during this phase of sleep, experienced in exaggerated form, while traces left by more intense impressions are experienced in very diminished form. Thus, for instance, the sleeper may perceive faint sounds as deafening and barely hear loud sounds. In dreams the images of small objects may assume gigantic proportions, whereas those of truly large objects are reduced to insignificant dimensions.

And so the century-old study of sleep and dreams has led mankind from animistic beliefs to the exact experiments of Pavlov. It is impossible not to underline the fact that the unraveling of the physiological mechanisms of sleep and dreams is a major achievement of our own progressive science, whose materialism is the basic source of its successes.

One would assume that all false explanations of dreams had long ago been consigned to archives, but they still prevail, even among educated men, if they are not fully cognizant of the achievements of modern natural science.

Anyone who has not yet discarded all superstition is especially amazed by the fantastic aspect of dreams. How often, on awaking, we ask ourselves, "Why did I dream this? Nothing like it exists. I have never heard, read, or conceived anything in the least like it!" Indeed, why do dreams so often bear no resemblance at all to anything that we can recall from our personal experience? The question is complicated, but science has an exhaustive answer.

First, it is possible to see in dreams what eluded our notice when we were awake. In support of this the French scholar, Delage, cites the following: An ornament, a glass globe, which used to stand on the staircase of his residence, broke and was not replaced for a long time. One night Delage dreamt that a metal ornament, in the shape of a fir-cone, had been substituted for the globe. In the morning he related his dream to his family; to his great amazement he learned that in fact a fir-cone such as he had seen in his dream had several days earlier replaced the globe. Since, from his dream, Delage had described the fir-cone exactly, he had no doubt seen it several times before this dream, but without paying attention to it. Later, on the stairs, he saw that the ornament was indeed real.

Secondly, once-remembered impressions that appear to have been completely erased from memory may be revived in dreams. When such unnoticed or forgotten images appear in dreams, we do not recognize them, they seem alien to us, evoked by some mysterious power. This is true to an even greater extent of dream images that "telescope" a number of different impressions from various periods of life. One investigator of dreams, for instance, dreamt of a female acquaintance. But in his dream she appeared to be very small (he had not long before seen a dwarf in the street) and her eyes slanted, as in a statuette of a Japanese divinity (which he had seen in an antique shop). The result was a fantastic image that never existed in reality.

I. M. Sechenov most aptly described this feature of dreams: "Dreams are frequently an unprecedented combination of ordinary impressions." And Pavlov wrote: "Dreams are usually a chain of varied, contradictory, trace stimulations."[7]

It must be remembered once and for all that, however wondrous, incomprehensible, and mysterious dreams may seem, they contain only what we have experienced, consciously or unconsciously, at least once in our waking state. Dreams are nothing more than the reprocessing by a partially awake brain of erratically tangled fragments and traces of some past experience, of what we, at one time or another, had seen, heard, thought, or read.

This basic principle underlying the study of dreams is frequently disputed by those who are still predisposed to see something mysterious in them. If what you say is true, they counter, then why do we so often fly in dreams? In the real world none of us has ever flown. This question may be answered as follows: we have all watched the flight of birds, butterflies, bats; during sleep we transfer this experience to

[7] Cited in F. P. Mayorov, *Fiziologicheskaya teoria snovideniy* (The Physiological Theory of Dreams), Moscow and Leningrad: AN, SSSR, 1951, p. 39.

ourselves. The circumstances which evoke such dreams are well known. They occur when, after being impeded, the sleeper's respiration suddenly becomes free and easy. It has been demonstrated that, if a sleeper's head is covered by a blanket, which is subsequently removed, this sleeper will later often announce that he had a flying dream. Just as simple is the explanation of another "strange" dream — falling into an abyss. A man falls asleep with his knees bent; if his legs are quickly straightened for him he will dream that he is falling. And he will have the same dream if he himself unconsciously performs the act of straightening.

A mystical meaning is frequently attributed to so-called "creative dreams." It is known that many famous people perceived in dreams the solution to problems with which they had wrestled unsuccessfully during their waking hours. Mathematical problems have been solved in this manner. The German chemist, Kekule von Stradonitz, perceived in a dream the structural formula of a complex chemical substance — benzene. Voltaire saw in a dream a new version of his poem "Henriade." The Italian composer, Tartini, wrote some of his sonatas after having first heard them played by others in a dream. The German physiologist, K. Burdach, V. M. Bekhterev, and many other scientists reported that some of their new ideas originated in dreams. There is nothing extraordinary about these cases. They merely indicate that the sleep of people immersed in creative work is frequently incomplete: the areas of the cerebral cortex which worked most strenuously during the day are not fully inhibited, remain in a state of excitation, and continue to work at night.

For many, the alleged prophetic and oracular purport of dreams remains their most mysterious aspect even today. We have already cited several "diagnostic" dreams that presaged illness, proving in their analysis that there was nothing prophetic in them. Such dreams are, by the way, rare. "Prophetic dreams" are more often founded simply on misunderstanding. Nearly everyone has dreams, sometimes many dreams in one night. In a week, a month, a person accumulates tens, if not hundreds, of dreams. Do many of them materialize? Of course not. Dreams as a rule do not materialize; only in exceptional cases do they coincide, more or less, with future events. According to the theory of probability this is as it should be: many dreams, many events — some of them must inevitably coincide. There is nothing wonderful in this. But the superstitious person is so constituted that he attaches greater significance to rare coincidences than to the habitual absence of such coincidences. If we believe that some aspect of a dream we have seen corresponds to an event that occurs a day, two days, a week, or a month later, we sound the alarm, and recount it as a marvel, naively losing sight of the fact that tens or hundreds of other dreams failed to coincide with the events of our life.

Belief in the prophetic meaning of dreams is one of the most stubborn illusions of the human mind, and further reinforced by coincidence of another kind. It was long ago observed that longings and desires, whether open or hidden, are fulfilled in dreams. A child, tempted by the great quantities of candy he sees displayed in a store's showcase, asks for some, but the mother refuses to gratify his plea. Later the child, still full of his unrealized desire, finds it difficult to fall asleep, and dreams that his desire is at last gratified; he sees himself in the store, taking all the candy he wants. Adults, too, frequently have the same experience: seeking fulfillment of some secret desire, we see this desire realized in a dream; later, when after a great deal of effort we finally attain our goal, we recall the dream, are astonished, and declare it to have been "prophetic."

The Austrian psychiatrist, Sigmund Freud, devoted much study to the psychological analysis of dreams. According to his findings, expounded in his comprehensive work, *The Interpretation of Dreams,* many dreams are engendered by sensual urges — once experienced consciously, but now suppressed and "repressed" from the conscious sphere into a "subconscious" one — by forbidden desires, unrealized or unrealizable, and the highly disturbing images, predominantly sexual, associated with them. We are no longer aware of these seemingly forgotten experiences; nonetheless, they continue to affect our behavior and mood, and may provoke baseless fears, agitation, and so forth. These "repressed complexes" — clots of repressed images and emotions — emerge over and over again from the depths of the subconscious psychic sphere only in dreams, so that they may, so to speak, be gradually disposed of in coded, symbolic, form. Despite the idealistic orientation of Freud's theoretical views, which is not acceptable to us, there is, apparently, a grain of truth in his empirical investigation of dreams. The Soviet psychiatrist, I. A. Perepel,[8] made an attempt, which is worth our attention, to translate Freud's

---

[8] See his *Psikhoanaliz i fiziologicheskaya teoria povedenia* (Psychoanalysis and the Physiological Theory of Behavior), Leningrad, 1928.

psychological theories into the language of modern physiological thought concerning higher nervous activity. Similar attempts are being made today.[9]

No one disputes any longer the existence of unconscious or subconscious phenomena. Even the philosophers who reject Freud's theories from the new point of dialectical materialism write: "On one point Freud is correct: the unconscious. It exists, it functions, and it influences the conscious process. It accomplishes this not in terms of some "purely physiological," conditioned nervous connections which are from time to time inhibited, but is really a living sphere, full of *meaningfulness,* whose influence all of us have sensed. That which we know but do not at the moment recall has a definite *meaningful* content which in principle is not reducible to the excitation or inhibition of the cortical cells." (Author's italics).[10]

Either too much significance has been attributed to dreams, or, conversely, they were declared to be devoid of significance and interest. Both these extremes are incorrect. Dreams may exert considerable influence on our mood the next day. This is especially true of nightmares, which leave an emotional imprint on the daily activity of the healthy, and have an even greater impact on sick people (neuropaths). Noting these facts in his book, Professor F. P. Mayorov[11] cites

---

[9] See E. Sh. Ayrapetnyants and K. M. Bykov, *Uchenie ob interotseptsii i psikhologia podsoznatelnovo* (The Theory of Interoception and the Psychology of the Subconscious), p. 273 (*Uspekhi sovremennoy biologii* [Progress in Modern Biology]), vol. XV, 1942; H. Wells, *Pavlov i Freyd* (Pavlov and Freud), Moscow: IL, 1959.

[10] F. Mikhaylov and G. Tsaregorodzev, *Za porogom soznania: kriticheskiy ocherk freydianisma* (Beyond the Threshold of the Conscious: A Critical Essay on Freudianism), Gospolizdat, 1961, p. 45.

[11] *Fiziologicheskia teoria snovideniy* (The Physiological Theory of Dreams), p. 122.

as his authority V. M. Bekhterev, who asserted that dreams may influence our frame of mind "in the same way that unusual suggestions influence it." Nor, as we have seen, can one deny the occasional diagnostic significance of dreams. One of the outstanding Soviet neuropathologists, M. I. Astvatsaturov, wrote in this connection:

"It can, for instance, be acknowledged that, in the absence of any other subjective complaints indicating such an illness, when alarming dreams, containing an element of the fear of death in them, are combined with sudden awakening, such dreams may arouse the suspicion of an ailing heart."[12]

Parapsychologists do not concur in the assertion that in dreams it is possible for the sleeper to see only fragments and traces of what he has personally experienced, only that which he at one time or another saw, heard, thought, or read. Avowing the existence of telepathic and telesthetic phenomena, they assume that some dreams may be conditioned by parapsychological abilities, which are intensified during both natural and hypnotic sleep.

In order not to repeat myself, I refer the reader to my book, *Mental Suggestion at a Distance*,[13] in which a number of such dreams, interpreted by the parapsychologists as "telepathic," are cited. Here I shall confine myself to only one example of an alleged telesthetic (clairvoyant) dream, taken from Ch. Richet's treatise.[14]

---

[12] *Sovetskaya vrachebnaya gazeta*, No. 1 (1939), p. 10.

[13] *Vnushenie na rasstoyanii: zametki fiziologa* (Suggestion at a Distance: A Physiologist's Notes), Gospolizdat, 1962. See Ch. II, "Sluchai iz obydennoy zhizni, prinimayemye za vnushenie na rasstoyanii" (Common Incidents Interpreted as Suggestion at a Distance).

[14] *Traité de métapsychique*, Paris, 1923, p. 153.

There lived in Havre a certain Léonie B., a neurotic noted for her parapsychological abilities. She was the subject of many experiments by Dr. Gilbert and Professors Janet and Richet. Once, when Richet and Gilbert were in Paris, Janet put Léonie into a hypnotic sleep and suggested to her that in her dream she should go to Paris to see Richet and Gilbert. Suddenly the subject announced, "There is a fire there." Janet tried to calm her, but she continued to assert: "But I assure you, M. Janet, there is a fire there." Later Janet learned that on that very day, November 15, at six o'clock in the morning, a fire had destroyed Professor Richet's laboratory. Janet had put Léonie into her hypnotic sleep at precisely 7 P.M. of the same day, which was before anyone in Havre, including Janet, could have known about the fire.[15]

An analogous incident (which is perhaps more significant) occurred with the same subject, but this time she was awake. One evening, after several unsuccessful attempts at mental suggestion with numbers and playing cards, Richet asked Léonie B.:

"What is M. Langlois [director of the laboratory where Richet had worked when he was young] doing?"

She quickly answered: "He has burned his hand. Why was he so careless when pouring?"

"Pouring what?"

"Some red fluid into a small flask... His skin swelled immediately."

"One couldn't have expressed it more precisely," wrote

---

[15] This incident occurred in the mid-eighties of the last century, when communication between cities was still poor.

Richet. It turned out that two hours earlier, Langlois, in pouring bromine into a flask while conducting a chemical experiment, had been in a hurry and careless. This "red fluid" spilled on his hand and forearm, instantly forming a rather large blister. Léonie had no access to the laboratory, and no one there had as yet seen Richet.

In similar incidents one cannot exclude the possibility of two totally unrelated events coinciding by chance. Consequently, such incidents are not in themselves sufficient proof of the existence of telepathic and clairvoyant perceptions or dreams. Accounts of such occurrences will become truly significant only when telepathic and telesthetic phenomena are confirmed by repeated experiments, which we shall discuss in chapters VI and VII.

Hypnotism
and Suggestion

Hypnotism
and Suggestion

OF ALL THE NEUROPSYCHOLOGICAL PHENOMENA which have engendered, and still engender, superstitious talk, nocturnal sleep and dreams are the most common. Other varieties of sleep and twilight states of consciousness, which are encountered most frequently in hysterics, are incomparably rarer. Among them should be included lethargy — a deep pathological (morbid) sleep which may last many days, sometimes even weeks. During such sleep, not only voluntary movements but even simple reflexes are suppressed to such an extent, and the physiological functions of the respiratory organs and circulation of the blood reach so depressed a point, that it is possible for people with little medical knowledge to mistake the sleeper for dead.

Fear of being buried alive was especially strong in the eighteenth and beginning of the nineteenth centuries. There circulated at the time a work entitled *Instructions for the Care of the Dead*, compiled by Dr. Tari. In this unique document we may read the following: "Inasmuch as there are instances of hysterical, allegedly dead women returning to life even after so long an interval as six days...it would serve a useful purpose to build houses of the dead in every cemetery. Special inspectors should examine the body several times a day. The dead should be left on a bed, covered with a blanket, with nose, mouth, and eyes left uncovered. The room should be aired frequently...[and] fumigated with vinegar, poured on hot stones, for acid fumes are good even for the bodies of healthy people, and with such the electricizing of the body takes effect better...These measures would provide the best precautions against premature burials."[1] As is evident from the above, in determining whether a person was really dead or in lethargic sleep, there were already attempts to apply electric current, obtained not long before by the Italian physicist, Volta, by means of the so-called "Volta's pile."

The following is a typical example of lethargic sleep. "Dr. Rosenthal of Vienna published an account of the trance of a female hysteric, whom the attending doctor had pronounced dead. When Rosenthal saw her, her skin was ashen and cold, her pupils contracted and insensitive to light, her pulse imperceptible, and her extremities limp. Hot sealing wax dripped on her skin did not evoke the slightest reflex movement. A mirror was applied to her mouth: no trace of moisture could be observed on its surface. It was impossible to discern the least respiratory sound, but auscultation in the region of the heart revealed a barely perceptible intermittent murmur. The patient

---

[1] From the German book by Professor G. Halle, *Magic or the Magical Power of Nature* (Russian translation published by the University of Moscow, Khr. Klaud, 1801), pp. 354-59.

had already been in this apparently lifeless state for thirty-six hours. On examining the patient with intermittent electric current, Rosenthal found that the muscles of the face and extremities contracted. The patient recovered after a twelve-hour faradization (treatment with electric current). Two years later she was still alive and well, and told Rosenthal that at the inception of the attack she had lost all consciousness, but later could hear the conversation about her death, without in any way being able to help herself."[2]

The American writer, Edgar Allan Poe, who depicted various horrors in his literary works, assembled a whole collection of "premature burial" stories. It is possible that in the past such tragic incidents did actually occur now and then, and their impact on superstitious people was unnerving. This fact is, in all likelihood, the source of one of the most gloomy and absurd fictions — belief in the existence of vampires and werewolves; that is, the belief that people who died an "unreal death" are able to leave their graves and crypts at night in order to sustain their half-alive, half-dead existence with the blood of the living.

Today the various forms of prolonged sleep, which sometimes lasts many years, have been well studied, and the superstitions associated with them have been relegated to the realm of legends. Following are two remarkable examples of such prolonged sleep.

---

[2] Cited by Dr. Braid, *"Sushchnost i yavlenia transa"* (The Nature and Phenomena of the Trance), in D. I. Mendeleev, *Materialy dlya suzhdenia o spiritisme* (Materials for the Appraisal of Spiritualism), St. Petersburg, 1876, p. 294.

In France a neurotically sick four-year-old girl was frightened by something, fainted, then sank into a lethargic sleep which lasted eighteen consecutive years. She was put in a hospital, where she was carefully nursed and fed; thanks to this care, she grew up. But, though she was an adult when she woke up, her mind, interests, and feelings had not developed beyond the stage they had reached just before she fell asleep. Thus, on awakening from the lethargy, she asked for a doll to play with.[3] I. P. Pavlov knew a case of an even more prolonged sleep. For twenty-five years a man remained a "living corpse" in a clinic. He did not make a single motion nor speak a single word from the age of thirty-five to the age of sixty, when he gradually began to reveal normal motor activity — began to get up, speak, and so on. The old man was questioned about how he felt during his long years as a "living corpse." It turned out that he heard, saw, and understood much, but could neither move nor speak. Pavlov attributed this to stagnant pathological inhibition of the motor region of the cerebral cortex. At the inception of old age, when the inhibitory processes weaken, cortical inhibition began to abate, and the old man woke up.[4]

There are well-known accounts by European travelers and Indian writers of Indian yogis who, by use of certain methods of autohypnosis known to them, and breath control, are able to induce in themselves at will a state of the deepest and most pro-

---

[3] V. V. Yefimov, *Son i snovidenia* (Sleep and Dreams), Moscow and Leningrad: Gostekhizdat, 1947, p. 8.
[4] S. I. Galperin, *Son i snovidenia* (Sleep and Dreams), Leningrad, 1945, pp. 12-13.

longed sleep, similar to lethargy or catalepsy. L. Levenfeld, in his book *Hypnotism,* devotes an entire chapter to this subject.[5]

He relates that, as long ago as 1893, G. Valter included in his dissertation a translation from the Sanscrit of an ancient Indian manuscript which described the exercises that enable yogis to induce prolonged sleep. These exercises consist primarily of the gradual prolongation of the period of holding the breath, which finally leads to a temporary cessation of the activity of consciousness. Simultaneously, the yogi assumes a comfortable position and, with head lowered and eyes half-open, "focuses his gaze on some point between the eyebrows," covers (or someone covers them for him) his nose, mouth, and ears, and "listens intently to his inner voice," which resembles either the tinkling of a bell, the murmur of a conch shell, the sound of a trumpet, or the buzzing of a bee. All these devices allegedly induce the deepest autohypnosis, which is similar to lethargy, "the seeming death of hysterical patients."

The Academician I. R. Tarkhanov was very much interested in this subject. In his book, *The Spirit and the Body* (which is of great interest even today), he writes that certain Europeans, too, succeeded, though to a lesser degree, in inducing something similar to the sleep of the yogi — with this difference: instead of holding the breath they practiced checking the beating of the heart by will power. This is what he writes in this connection:

"However difficult it is to imagine that the heart or the blood vessels should submit to the will, as do our skeletal muscles, nevertheless medical literature cites instances that

---

[5] *Gipnotism* (Hypnotism), Saratov, 1903, pp. 186-89.

apparently indicate the existence of some such possibility. Thus Bell [an English physiologist] was able to retard to a significant degree the beating of his heart at will... Chermak [another noted physiologist] was able to retard and stop the beating of his heart. Finally, medical literature mentions a certain English colonel, Townsend, who could at will stop the beating of his heart for so long a time that he would fall into a faint; during such attempts his body grew cold and stiff, his eyes became fixed, and he finally lost all consciousness; after several hours in this state he would gradually recover his senses [like the yogi]. For a long time these demonstrations had no ill effects; finally, however, after performing such an experiment before a number of witnesses, he died the evening of the same day."[6]

As is well-known, hypothermy, that is, the gradual cooling of the body of the person to be operated on until he reaches a state comparable to the winter sleep of certain animals — for instance, marmots, bats, and others — is widely used in modern surgery.[7]

Another variety of pathological sleep, called lunatism, sleepwalking, or natural somnambulism has also been known a long time. A healthy man who dreams that he is going somewhere or is performing some task remains motionless. A sleepwalker, on the other hand, though he continues to sleep, leaves the bed, takes a walk, or automatically performs the task he has dreamt about. After executing his task, he returns

---

[6] I. R. Tarkhanov, *"Dukh i telo"* (The Spirit and the Body), Supplement to *Vestnik i biblioteka samoobrazovania*, St. Petersburg, 1904, p. 110.

[7] See the article by V. Burakovsky, *"Gipotermia"* (Hypothermy), *Bolshaya meditsinskaya entsiklopedia*, VII, 1958, pp. 244-50.

to bed and sleeps tranquilly until morning; when he awakes, he remembers nothing of the night's adventures. Here is an authentic account of a well-educated man who was afflicted with somnambulism:

"One night he was discovered translating Italian into French; he was poring over a dictionary and selecting words by the light, ostensibly, of an adjacent candle. When the candle was extinguished, he searched for it and relit it. This was totally unnecessary, for the room was illuminated by other lighted candles, which he did not see, because he was not aware that they were lit."[8]

Natural somnambulism, which is a fairly frequent phenomenon, may have given rise to the ancient superstition about the existence of a house "spirit"— the brownie. At night, when everyone in the house is asleep, this benevolent spirit allegedly does the various household chores left unfinished by the masters. Actually, it may have been a member of the family suffering from somnambulism who finished the chores.

In addition to somnambulists who in their sleep continue their customary activities, there are somnambulists who while asleep do things that are completely alien to them when they are awake. These cases aroused the interest of the eminent Russian biologist I. I. Mechnikov. He described the following occurrence:

One of the Paris hospitals hired as nurse a twenty-four-

---

[8] A. Lehmann, *Illustrirovannaya istoria sueveriy i volshebstva ot drevnosti do nashikh dney* (Illustrated History of Superstitions and Magic from Ancient to Modern Times), Moscow, 1900, p. 489.

year-old hysteric who turned out to be a somnambulist. One
night the doctor on duty observed the following:

The young woman got up from the bed and went up to
the garret which contained the dormitory where she had
formerly slept. On reaching the top landing, she opened the
window leading to the roof, stepped through, and started to
walk along the ledge in sight of another nurse, who watched
her, terrified, but did not dare speak; then she returned through
a different window, and started down the stairs. "At that moment we saw her," the doctor on duty related. "She was walking
noiselessly, her movements were automatic, and her arms hung
alongside her slightly bent body; she held her head erect and
motionless; her hair was loose, her eyes wide open. She looked
like some fantastic apparition."[9]

According to Mechnikov, cases of this type are "sufficient
testimony that when he is in a state of natural somnambulism,
man acquires faculties he does not normally possess, and that
*he becomes a strong, agile, excellent gymnast, comparable in
all respects to his anthropoid ancestors* . . . Man inherited from
his ancestors many brain mechanisms whose functions were
suppressed by subsequently developed inhibitory processes."[10]
During somnambulistic states these ancient brain mechanisms
are disinhibited, to a greater or lesser degree, through inhibition of those cortical areas acquired later and present only in
man. "For this reason," Mechnikov concludes, "we may assume
that *the gymnastic feats and astonishing strength of somnambulists are a reversion to the animal state*,"[11] a return to the in-

---

[9] I. I. Mechnikov, *Etyudy optimizma* (Optimistic Sketches), Moscow,
1913, p. 183.
[10] Ibid., p. 186.   [11] Ibid., p. 187.

stincts manifested by climbing animals, man's nearest ancestors.

Mechnikov's hypothesis clearly echoes Pavlov's views on dreams, already cited; as a result of the inhibition of the highest, and phylogenetically much more recent, functions of the cerebral cortex, there occurs during ordinary sleep disinhibition of the (phylogenetically older) more primitive type of connections, so-called thinking restricted to objects and images; and during somnambulistic sleep even more ancient motor automatisms, presumably lost by modern man, are released.

In rare cases a somnambulistic state may last weeks or months, then suddenly the somnambulist returns to normality. An astonishing phenomenon has been observed in such cases: the splitting of consciousness into primary — normal — and secondary somnambulistic states. The following is one of the remarkable examples of this phenomenon:

A girl named Felida was born to healthy parents. The first symptoms of hysteria appeared when she was thirteen. They were followed, a year and a half later, by attacks of hysterical somnambulism. In time the attacks became less frequent, but the duration of the secondary, somnambulistic, psychic state lengthened. When Felida was thirty-two, the latter state would last nearly three months, with sporadic interruptions of a few hours by the normal, primary, state. The secondary, or somnambulistic, personality remembered clearly the events that had occurred during both phases, but the primary, or normal, personality did not recall any of the activities it had engaged in during its somnambulistic phase. For this reason, Felida, during the last years of her life, greatly disliked the brief flashes of the normal phase. It was easier for her to live with the secondary personality than with the first. This was reflected in her character. During the period of normality she was depressed, withdrawn, silent, complained constantly of pain, was preoccupied solely with herself, and paid little heed to her surroundings. During the state of somnambulism she was gay and carefree, disliked working, and spent more time on her appearance; on the other hand, she was more affectionate and tender toward children and kin. Thus, indubitably, two personalities existed in one person![12]

Drastic changes in personality sometimes occur very suddenly, as a result of some strong mental shock. The noted French psychologist, A. Binet, described the following typical case: A sixteen-year-old youth worked in a vineyard. Once, while at work, he stumbled on a snake. The shock was so great that he fainted. When he came to, his legs were paralyzed. This was supplemented by profound psychic changes. The youth thought that he was a nine-year-old boy, and behaved accordingly. He read badly, wrote like a beginner, and lived exclusively with the impressions and interests of a nine-year-old. The last segment of his life was entirely forgotten, and his later-acquired life experiences were all lost. Because of his paralyzed legs he was transferred from the vineyard to a tailoring workshop. There he learned to sew, relearned reading and writing, and became a tailor. Several years later our tailor suffered another strong mental shock, which resulted in a long faint. When he came to this time, his legs were no longer paralyzed and he remembered the previously forgotten segment of his life and his work in the vineyard before the encounter

---

[12] See L. Levenfeld, *Gipnotism,* pp. 247-48.

with the snake. On the other hand, he no longer remembered anything of his life in the tailoring shop. Forgotten, too, was all his tailoring knowledge and skill.

In his lectures N. E. Vvedensky pointed out that these, so to speak, transformations from one personality to another were most skillfully depicted by Dostoyevsky. The great psychological writer was very much interested in these phenomena. One may cite first of all the ludicrous introspections of the poor civil councilor, Pralinsky, who, in *A Ribald Anecdote,* suddenly gets drunk at the wedding supper of one of his subordinates; then the series of scenes and events described in *The Eternal Husband;* and finally the development of an outright split personality in Golyadkin in *The Double* and in Ivan Fyodorovich in *The Brothers Karamazov.* These examples from Dostoyevsky demonstrate that different degrees of split personality are not too rare a phenomenon in the ordinary lives of so-called healthy people.

When nervous and psychic illnesses were still a complete enigma, such phenomena were interpreted as "possession," as the periodic entrance into the body of the patient of some alien personality, most frequently the personality of some restless soul unable to find a place for itself in the world beyond the grave. One would think that so absurd a notion would long ago have been consigned to the realm of legends; instead, it bloomed luxuriantly anew in the twentieth century, in the form of so-called spiritualism. The heroes of spiritualistic séances are the mediums who, at the persuasion of the spirits, serve as intermediaries between the living and the souls of the dead. Falling into a trance (a type of pathological sleep) during séances, the mediums speak, write, and act in the name of the "spirit" who is "controlling" them, usually the "spirit" of some famous dead person or a deceased relative of one of the people present. If the medium is not simply a liar (which is a fact in the majority of cases), he is a sick man afflicted with a distinctive split personality, in which case the onset of his pathological condition is induced by the whole mysterious atmosphere of the séance.[13]

The "mystery" of these and other similarly remarkable phenomena was dissipated like smoke when scientists, in their experiments with neurotic patients, learned to reproduce them artificially by means of hypnosis and mental suggestion.

The history of hypnotism may be divided into three periods. The first belongs to hoary antiquity. There is no doubt that hypnotic sleep was already known to the Egyptian and Greek priests. This is attested by the so-called "gnostic papyrus" (second century B.C.), which describes methods of hypnotism still in use even today. The priests utilized hypnotism for religious purposes. Usually questions were put to some young votary of the temple who had first been plunged into a deep hypnotic sleep; his answers were then interpreted as instructions from the gods, as prophecy. In ancient Greece hypnotism was used also for medical purposes. This is indicated by the legends, still available to us, concerning the celebrated god of healing of antiquity, Aesculapius.

During the Middle Ages, the scanty knowledge of the ancients concerning hypnotic sleep was lost, and the methods of hypnotizing forgotten. Scientific interest in hypnotic phe-

---

[13] For more details, see Ch. V.

nomena revived only at the beginning of the Renaissance. Hypnotism was first used in experiments on animals. Thus, in the first half of the seventeenth century, the press reported the "bewitched state of a chicken": "the miraculous experiment" performed by the German scientists, Schwenter and Kircher. The essence of the matter is as follows: holding the chicken firmly in his hands, the experimenter carefully presses its head to the floor, leaving it in this position for some time in order to induce in it an immobile, limp condition similar to that of deep sleep, from which it can be aroused only by a rude jolt or loud noise.

In their zeal to explain such phenomena, the contemporary scientists promulgated a fantastic theory. This theory, which is characteristic of the second period in the history of hypnotism, is known as animal magnetism.

Paracelsus, a famous contemporary physician, and his followers, Van Helmont and Fludd, asserted that one person could influence the organism and psyche of another through some mysterious "life force" which allegedly emanates from the arms, eyes, and other bodily organs. This alleged force, or emanation, was at first called "fluid." Later, however, the notion spread that the influence exerted by the "fluid" on living creatures was comparable to the effect produced by the common magnet, to which medicinal powers were attributed at the time. Consequently, the "fluid" was rechristened "animal magnetism," and persons with the ability to transfer their curative magnetism to patients began to be called "magnetizers."

In the second half of the eighteenth century this far-from-true theory was definitively formulated and disseminated by the Viennese physician, Mesmer, whose reputation as the founder of hypnotism is hardly justified. By the use of various processes which stimulate the imagination, such, for instance, as passing his hands over the body of the patient in order allegedly to transfer his own magnetism to that patient (so-called "passes"), Mesmer provoked a state of "crisis"—a hysterical attack, expressed in twitchings, convulsions, piercing shrieks, and uncontrollable laughter or weeping. According to his "theory," every nervous disease had to be artificially brought to a climax in order for the body to heal. The violent patients, in the throes of "crisis," were carried by Mesmer's assistants to the "hall of crises," filled with carpets and featherbeds, where, on coming back to themselves, they did sometimes indeed recover from their illnesses.

In 1774, a commission for the investigation of animal magnetism was formed in Paris. It was composed of the most prominent scientists from the faculties of the University of Paris and the French Academy of Sciences, and headed by Franklin and Lavoisier. The commission made a thorough investigation of the medical activities of Mesmer and his follower, Deslon, and devised a number of ingenious experiments designed to solve the "animal-magnetism-fluid" question. These experiments conclusively disproved the existence of such a fluid. At the same time they led to an important discovery by demonstrating what a powerful physiological effect an excited imagination may exert. Everything that Mesmer and his followers attributed to the influence of magnetic fluid, the commission explained as being effected by imagination (this term was later replaced by the terms "suggestion" and "autosuggestion"). Below is an excerpt from the concluding remarks of this commission, which played so important a role in the history of the struggle against superstition.

"The Commission having found that animal magnetic fluid is inaccessible to any of our five senses, that it has not the slightest effect on either the members of the Commission or the patients whom the Commission has submitted to its influence;... having finally shown by supportive experiments that the imagination without the aid of magnetism can produce convulsions, and that magnetism without the imagination can produce nothing; it has come to the following unanimous conclusions... [concerning] the existence and utility of animal magnetism: that there is no proof of the existence of the animal magnetic fluid; that this fluid, having no existence, has in consequence no utility; but that the morbid effects which are observed in public treatment are caused by touching, excited imagination, and the mechanical imitation which forces us involuntarily to repeat that which surprises us..."[14]

How great a power was attributed to the imagination by Lavoisier is clear from the following: "We encounter the influence of magnetism, or rather, the imagination, in the theatre, at war, at mass riots, among the crowds at the curative baths (Mesmer's); this power is active everywhere, and terrifying; its manifestations amaze us, while its source remains dark and mysterious."[15]

---

[14] *Ouevres de Lavoisier*, 1865, III, pp. 513-27. Russian translation in D. I. Mendeleev, *Materialy dlya suzhdenia o spiritisme*, p. 227. [English translation from Frank Podmore, *From Mesmer to Christian Science* (New Hyde Park, N. Y.: University Books, 1963), p. 59 — Tr.]
[15] Mendeleev, ibid., p. 275.

Nevertheless, in the history of science the honor of the second discovery of hypnotism does not belong to Mesmer, but to his pupil and follower, Puységur. The following is a description of this accidental discovery by a historian of mesmerism:

"Out of dilettantish humanism and philosophical interest he [Puységur] conducts at his estate free magnetic treatments in accordance with the precepts of his patron. Once a whole group of people seeks his help, and the count-philanthropist[16] tries to arouse in his patients the most violent crises possible. Suddenly he's astounded, more than that — frightened. Instead of reacting to the magnetic passes with twitchings, convulsions, and spasms, a young shepherd, called Victor, discloses only fatigue and falls peacefully asleep. Since such behavior is contrary to the rule according to which the magnetizer must first of all produce not sleep but convulsions, Puységur tries to rouse the bumpkin. In vain! Puységur shouts at him — the man does not move. He shakes him, but wonder of wonders: this stocky fellow's sleep is not ordinary sleep, not normal sleep. And suddenly, when Puységur once more orders him to get up, the lad does so and takes a few steps, but with his eyes shut. Nevertheless, despite the closed lids, he functions as if he were awake, as a man in possession of all his senses; yet he continues to sleep. He, in broad daylight, fell into a state of somnambulism, and begins to wander in his sleep. The embarrassed Puységur tries to talk to him, asks him questions. What happens? The peasant lad in his sleepy state answers every question intelligently and clearly. Excited by this strange phenome-

---

[16] Puységur was a marquis — Tr.

non, Puységur repeats the experiment. And succeeds, by means of magnetic methods, in evoking a similar state of being asleep and awake at the same time not only in the young shepherd but in many others as well. Greatly agitated by this unexpected discovery, he redoubles his efforts. He makes what is known as posthypnotic suggestions, that is, orders the sleeper to execute a series of specific tasks upon awakening. And on their return to normal consciousness the patients do indeed execute the tasks suggested to them while they were asleep."[17]

But, though they had learned how to bring on somnambulistic attacks by artificial means, and were able to plunge their patients into hypnotic sleep, Mesmer's followers misunderstood these phenomena entirely. At the time, European science still knew nothing about suggestion, which, as it turned out, is precisely the factor that induces a hypnotic state. Only at the beginning of the nineteenth century did the Portuguese abbot, Faria, who had spent many years in India, where hypnotic phenomena had been known since antiquity, begin to demonstrate in Europe experiments in verbal hypnotism without any passes, hence without the influence on the hypnotized subjects of some imaginary magnetic fluid. In the forties of the last century, the English surgeon, Braid, perfected the method of verbal hypnotism and supplemented it by the following auxiliary method: the subject was asked to fix his gaze upon some brilliant object (fixation tires the eyes of the subject; this helps the verbal suggestion of sleep).

It should be noted that Braid was skeptical about mes-

---

[17] Stefan Zweig, *Vrachevanie i psikhika* (Medical Treatment and the Psyche), Leningrad, 1932, pp. 97-98. (Translated from the German.)

merism. However, in an effort to expose the supposedly clever frauds of the Swiss magnetizer, Lafontaine, he became convinced of the authenticity of the hypnotic phenomena demonstrated by the latter and began to study the subject. He conclusively disproved the "magnetic-fluid theory" and substituted the modern term "hypnotism" (from the Greek *hypnos* — sleep) for the term "animal magnetism." Finally, Braid pioneered the use of hypnotic sleep in painless surgery. These contributions entitle him to the honor of being considered the true founder of hypnotism's third, now thoroughly scientific, line of advance.

The British physician's researches met with little success among his contemporaries. Hypnotism and verbal therapy seemed no less a miracle than hypnotism and therapy by means of a magnetizer's fluid. Among his scientific colleagues, Braid's verbal suggestions evoked visions of the magic exorcisms of bygone days. It was now necessary to convince his contemporaries that there was nothing mysterious or miraculous in the act of suggestion, that is, in the influence exerted by words on man's neuro-psychic condition. This problem was resolved by subsequent researchers who showed that the mere thought of some movement may bring on the same movement in the subject, against his will. For instance: if one stands behind the subject, who is completely awake, and persistently reiterates that he's not steady on his feet, that he's being dragged backwards, the subject, if he is sufficiently suggestible, will begin to totter more and more, to lose his equilibrium, and may eventually fall down. And if a suggested thought of some movement leads to involuntary execution of that movement, then there is nothing astonishing in the fact that a thought of sleep suggested by a hypnotist should induce real sleep. Thus, hypnotism proved to be nothing more than induced sleep, brought on by the subject's thought of the act of falling asleep.

In the second half of the last century all these researches finally paved the way for the general acceptance of hypnotism and of its importance for medicine. A modest provincial French physician, Liébeault, used hypnotic methods of treatment widely and selflessly, making no secret of his practice. His work attracted the attention of two medical authorities, the French Professors, Bernheim and Charcot. These daring and gifted investigators did more to promote the recognition and dissemination of hypnotism than anyone else. However, it soon became apparent that there were important differences in their points of view concerning the nature of hypnotism. Charcot conjectured that deep hypnosis, with all its accompanying phenomena, could be observed only in hysterics and was in itself an artificially induced pathological state. Bernheim maintained the opposite: that hypnosis could be evoked in perfectly healthy people and that it approximated natural night sleep. In Russia, Bekhterev founded hypnology (a special science devoted to the study of hypnosis and suggestion). He reconciled to a significant degree the dissenting opinions of Charcot and Bernheim and contributed much that was new to this field of knowledge. However, only Pavlov, through his theory of higher nervous activity, succeeded in revealing the physiological basis of hypnotism and suggestion.

It may be assumed that the noted physiologist's deep interest in hypnosis dates back to the inception of his scientific activity when, at the end of the seventies and beginning of the eighties of the last century, the young Pavlov worked in the laboratory of his distinguished teacher, the eminent German physiologist, R. Heidenhain. In describing these years Ivan Petrovich later wrote the following: "European society was at the time interested in the experiments of the professional hypnotist, Hansen. Heidenhain had seen these experiments in Breslau, quickly replicated them, and by so doing became, together with Charcot, one of the first to point out that the field of hypnosis is a field of profound practical significance and of great scientific importance. He then formulated a hypothesis about hypnosis — that it was effected by retardation [inhibition] of the activity of the higher centers caused by the weak, rhythmic stimulation of the cutaneous nerves of the face, or of the auditory or optical nerves, which adapt themselves to the onset of the hypnotic state — and in collaboration with Bubnov brought to this point of view a degree of experimental confirmation . . ."[18]

Heidenhain's pamphlet, which still bore the outmoded title, "Animal Magnetism,"[19] expounded the first strictly physiological investigation of hypnotic phenomena, which years later was continued and brilliantly completed by his student Pavlov.

The current techniques of inducing hypnotic sleep differ

---

[18] I. P. Pavlov, *Polnoe sobranie sochineniy* (Collected Works), Moscow and Leningrad, 1952, VI, p. 98.
[19] *Zhivotniy magnetism.* Russian translation of 4th German edition, ed. Pavlov, St. Petersburg, 1881.

little from the methods developed by the classicists — Braid, Charcot, Bernheim, and others. For hypnotizing human beings, verbal suggestion of a sleepy state remains the chief method. Pavlov explains the physiological bases of this method as follows: "Currently the common method [of hypnotizing] consists of the reiteration of words (spoken in a low, monotonous tone) that depict the physiological processes of the sleepy state. In essence, these words are, of course, conditioned stimuli, in all of us firmly associated with the sleepy state, and for this reason evoking it."[20] Verbal suggestion of sleep, in itself a monotonous auditory stimulus functioning through both the second and the first signal systems, is usually accompanied by other monotonously rhythmic or prolonged weak stimuli. Among these may be visual fixation on brilliant objects, the sounds of a metronome or buzzer, light stroking of the skin, or so-called passes — the method used in old-fashioned magnetism. Passes are repeated hand movements of the hypnotist in front of the face and along the body of the subject being put to sleep. The motions of the hypnotist's warm hands, without touching, produce a sensation in the subject's skin of being very gently massaged by warm waves of air. Currently, such hand movements are being successfully replaced by "passes of warm light," either from an electric heater or a blue electric bulb swinging from a cord.

Persons of heightened suggestibility (hysterics, alcoholics, and others) may be plunged into hypnotic sleep very quickly by use of sudden powerful stimuli. Charcot, for instance, banged on a gong; the sudden flashing of a bright light, a

---

[20] I. P. Pavlov, *Polnoe sobranie sochineniy,* 1951, IV, pp. 425-26.

commanding shout, the hypnotist's injunction of "sleep!" serve the same purpose.[21] The swift turning of an animal on its back, done by means of a special device, is a method used in experiments for hypnosis of animals.

How does hypnosis differ from normal sleep? During the process of hypnotization a unique psychological interrelation, known as "rapport," is established between the hypnotist and the subject. What does this mean? In a state of deep natural sleep, man is not receptive to external influences. His consciousness is, so to speak, isolated from the world around him. The subject who has been plunged into deep hypnosis pays no attention to where he is, does not react to external stimulation, does not answer questions of those present; at the same time he manifests a more sensitive receptivity toward everything connected with the person of the hypnotist. A hypnotized person hears only the voice of the hypnotist, answers only him; more importantly still, every word of the hypnotist gives rise to unusually vivid images in the mind of the hypnotized subject, images that can easily transform into illusions or hallucinations, or bring about automatic execution of motor acts. If the hypnotized subject is left to himself for a long time, individualized rapport with respect to the hypnotist gradually weakens, and can be terminated. The subject will no longer react to the hypnotist's presence, or reply to his questions. Disappearance of rapport signifies transition from the hypnotic state to the state of natural sleep. And sometime later the subject does indeed awake by himself, as if from natural sleep.

---

[21] For a more detailed account of these methods see P. I. Bul, *Tekhnika vrachebnovo gipnoza* (The Technique of Medical Hypnosis), Leningrad: Medgiz, 1955.

It is also possible to observe the reverse transition — from natural to hypnotic sleep. It is known that some people have a habit of talking in their sleep, uttering disjointed words and whole sentences. At such moments it is sometimes possible to establish verbal contact or rapport with the sleeper by means of careful questions touching upon what he is talking about. As soon as the sleeeper begins to answer, the goal of the experiment is reached: natural nocturnal sleep has gone over to hypnosis, the sleeper has become hypnotized, and the experimenter a hypnotist, who can manage through suggestions. In some countries parents resort to this practice, hoping by such hypnotic suggestion to break their children of bad habits or inclinations.

In Pavlov's opinion, hypnosis is a special kind of partial sleep. A limited area of the cerebral cortex, which is connected with perception of the hypnotist's voice and understanding of his verbal suggestions, continues to function, remaining on duty as a "sentry locus of excitation." All other divisions of the cortex are inhibited, at times even more deeply than during natural sleep.

Wrote Pavlov, "The language of the person who embarks on hypnotizing a given subject, who to a certain degree is developing cortical inhibition, brings on, in the course of concentrating the [verbal] stimulation in a definite narrow region according to a general law, a deep internal inhibition simultaneously and naturally ... thereby excluding in all the rest of the cerebral mass any competing influence whatsoever from all other present or past traces of excitation. This factor is responsible for the great, almost insuperable, power of suggestion as a stimulus during, and even after, hypnosis. Language maintains its influence even after hypnosis and remains independent of other stimuli. Language, furthermore, is immune to them, not being in connection with them from the moment of its first instillation in the cortex. The wide embraceiveness of language explains why suggestion can produce in a hypnotized person so many diverse actions, directed toward both the inner and outer world of man."[22]

The word "sleep!" affects the person being hypnotized as a hypnogenous (sleep-inducing) conditioned stimulus, related to the second signal system; the word "awake!" acts as a verbal signal disinhibiting the cortex. Something comparable occurs in the above-cited experiments of B. N. Birman: a dog falls asleep at the sound of the "inhibitory" tone "mi" and awakens at the sound of the rousing conditioned stimulus, the tone "do." The tone "mi" in this instance corresponds to the verbal signal "sleep!;" the tone "do," to the verbal signal "awake!"

Still another phenomenon observed in these experiments relates them even more closely to the hypnotic séance. The mere sight of the experimenter, who had put the dog to sleep many times through sounding the "inhibitory" tones of a harmonium, and the mere sound of his voice, gradually began to put the dog into a sleepy state. The experimenter had only to come into the room for the dog to fall asleep. The appearance in the room of other people, who had not participated in the experiments, had no sleep-inducing effect. For the experimental animal, the experimenter himself had been transformed into a

---

[22] I. P. Pavlov, *Polnoe sobranie sochineniy*, IV, p. 429.

conditioned hypnogenous stimulus. A somewhat comparable phenomenon occurs in oft-repeated hypnotic séances; at each succeeding séance the subject falls into hypnosis more and more quickly. Finally, the mere sight of the hypnotist in the setting where the séances usually take place acts in a hypnotizing manner. Hypnosis may be attained even in the absence of the hypnotist: a phonograph record, on which is recorded his intoned verbal suggestion of sleep, may be substituted for him. A single experiment of this type should suffice to dispel superstitious notions of a mysterious magnetic power exercised by the hypnotist over the person he is hypnotizing.

For a chosen subject to be successfully hypnotized, it is indispensable that this subject should be sufficiently suggestible while still awake; only then can the thought of sleep, suggested by the hypnotist, produce real sleep. Once hypnosis takes over and some degree of individualized rapport is established, the suggestibility of the subject is extremely heightened. Taking advantage of this, the hypnotist resorts to verbal suggestions of, for example, a therapeutic nature, convinced that they will be effective. The greater the ease with which the loci of sentry excitation are formed in his cerebral cortex, and the deeper the accompanying inhibition of all the remaining cortical divisions, the greater the suggestibility of the subject.

According to the findings of authoritative hypnologists, as high as 80 to 90 per cent of subjects are susceptible to hypnosis. However, no more than 20 to 25 per cent of this number can be put into so deep a hypnotic state that individualized rapport is established and all recollection of what was suggested by the hypnotist in the course of sleep is lost. Interestingly, the highest degree of receptivity to hypnosis is found in 7- to 14-year-old children; the lowest in old people. In general, persons who are not addicted to analyzing their experiences are the most suggestible. Hypnosis succeeds also with subjects who are completely ignorant of hypnotism and who have no idea of the results of the hypnotic methods being applied to them.

Hypnosis is, as it were, an intermediate link between natural sleep and various forms of pathological sleep; its manifestations vary in different subjects. In some it is distinguished by extreme languidness, a total enervation of the musculature. If one raises the arm of such a hypnotic, it instantly falls down again, heavily and helplessly. This type of subject answers the questions of the hypnotist reluctantly and not at once. It has frequently been observed that such a reaction is accompanied by hyperesthesia — heightened sensitivity of the sense organs. Subjects of this type can, for instance, hear the hypnotist's command even when uttered in a low whisper at the far end of the room; but their suggestibility is low and their awakening difficult. We have here a "lethargic type" of hypnosis, an artificially induced and relatively weak degree of lethargy.

Charcot, in his experiments with lethargics, observed a remarkable phenomenon, whose nervous mechanism is not clear even today, and which he named "neuromuscular superexcitability." If one presses a finger into that part of the skin traversed by any nerve, those muscles of the lethargic subject which are innervated by this nerve will go into a state of persistent contraction. For example: pressure on the radial nerve causes all the fingers to open; mechanical pressure on the medial nerve causes the fingers to close into a fist; pressure

on the ulnar nerve causes the hand to assume the so-called
benediction pose — the second and third fingers outstretched,
the others against the palm.

The experimental subject does not, as a rule, have any
idea of which nerves control what muscles of the hand, and
the hypnotist does not tell him. Consequently, neither external
suggestion nor autosuggestion plays a role in these experiments.
The phenomenon has an undeniable reflex character and
points to a very heightened excitability of those nerves and
nerve centers which cause muscular contraction. Pressure on
the same nerves of the same subjects when they are awake has
no effect.[23]

"Charcot's phenomenon" demonstrates — and this is why
it is important — that not all the phenomena observed in hypnosis are the result of suggestion and autosuggestion. In the
hypnotic state, functional changes of a purely physiological
origin, which are not necessarily linked to suggestion or autosuggestion, also occur in the organism. In maintaining this, the
physio-hypnological school of Charcot, Bekheterev, and Pavlov
diverges from the views of the psycho-hypnological school of
Bernheim and his followers, which reduce all hypnotic phenomena without fail to suggestion or autosuggestion. Animal
hypnosis, in many respects similar to that of man, is another
proof that a hypnotic state may arise even apart from verbal
suggestion.

The most characteristic aspect of the second group of

---

[23] For a more detailed account, see P. Rishe, *Klinicheskiy ocherk bolshoy
isterii ili isteroepilepsii* (A Clinical Account of Advanced Hysteria or
Hysteroepilepsy), Kiev, 1886, pp. 299-305.

hypnotics is the so-called "wax flexibility" of the bodily members. The hypnotist takes the sleeper's arm, raises it, and, without uttering a word, releases it. The arm remains in the position given it. The hypnotist changes the position of the arm (or leg), and each time it remains as if frozen in the air. One may impose any pose desired on the hypnotic, and he will maintain it for many minutes until signs of fatigue appear. This is the "cataleptic type" of hypnosis. However, instead of waxy flexibility some cataleptics exhibit a tendency toward stubborn contraction. For instance: when the arm of such a hypnotic is bent at the elbow, it requires great effort to unbend it; and after this is finally accomplished, the arm reassumes its previous bent position. In sharply expressed cases the entire musculature of the hypnotic may go into a state of stubborn rigidity. When this occurs it is possible to demonstrate a highly spectacular experiment, known as the cataleptic bridge. The subject is placed in a horizontal position between two chairs so that the back of his head rests on one, his heels on the other. The rigidity of the neck, back, and leg muscles causes the body to remain as if suspended in air between two support points. Appropriate suggestion may increase the cataleptic tension of the musculature still further, or, conversely, decrease it. Comparable phenomena, in varying degrees of expressiveness, occur independently also in hysterics or hysteroepileptics. There are well-known accounts of Indian fakirs, as well as early Christian ascetics, the so-called stylites, who could remain in a praying, or some other deliberately difficult-to-maintain position, for hours, without showing any visible signs of fatigue. It is possible that on such occasions they fell into, or induced in themselves, a state of cataleptic autohypnosis.

Muscular catalepsy is often observed in hypnotized animals. Their bodies, too, may be manipulated into unusual postures, in which they remain as if frozen; this is accompanied by loss of both cutaneous sensitivity and sensitivity to pain.

Cataleptic subjects are much more susceptible to suggestion than lethargic hypnotics. Not only is the motor sphere subject to the influence of suggestion, but also the sensory sphere. It is possible, for instance, to suggest insensitivity to strong odors, sharp tastes, and painful stimulation.

The highest degree of receptivity to suggestion is observed in hypnotics of the somnambulistic type. In contradistinction to lethargics and cataleptics, somnambulists manifest great mobility and psychic activity. Their entire behavior is reminiscent of the "sleepwalkers" whom we have already cited. They walk freely about the room, readily enter into conversation with the hypnotist, and dance, sing, write, and describe their experiences at his command. Their eyes are frequently open. To an inexperienced onlooker these subjects seem not to be asleep at all, although they are in deep hypnosis. Suggested illusions and hallucinations are especially characteristic of hypnotics of the somnambulistic type. Under the influence of corresponding suggestions they accept the odor of spirit of ammonia as the fragrance of a rose, a crust of bread as an orange, the noise made by the audience as music; the face of a relative may seem to them to be that of a stranger, or they mistake a stranger for an acquaintance, and so on. These are all various examples of illusions. In these cases the suggested idea is more powerful than perception of reality itself and alters it in the sleeper's consciousness.

The next step in the development of illusions is hallucinations: under the influence of suggestion somnambulists see, hear, and perceive that which is non-existent in reality. For example: the hypnotist knows that the subject's mother has long been dead. But he declares: "You are mistaken, your mother is alive. She is present in this room. She is coming toward you. Welcome her!" And the somnambulist "sees" the dead mother, welcomes her joyfully, plies her with questions, and behaves as if meeting a close relative after a long separation.

Such experiments with artificially induced visual hallucinations tear the veil of mystery from the "spooks" and "apparitions" that persons with deranged imaginations sometimes fancy they see when awake — a phenomenon which serves to sustain belief in existence of the dead beyond the grave. Autosuggestion, brought on by effects of some incident leading to superstitious fear or by persistent, grieving thoughts of a deceased near one, plays a large role in the appearance of hallucinations. Here is a typical example:

"I heard a noise in the corridor, and on looking, saw a man in dark clothes standing at the door. I was terribly frightened and ran into the adjacent room, where Father found me lying on the floor. I saw the man very clearly; he had long hair. I was eleven at the time, I had been doing my homework, but was very nervous. My imagination was disturbed by the figure of the man which had appeared before me; it seemed

I knew him and had not long before seen him in his grave. The sight of the corpse hit me hard; this was the reason for my nervousness. There was probably a perfectly natural reason for the sound I heard."[24]

In the days of universal belief in the existence of demons, pathological hallucinations frequently involved sexual relations with so-called incubi and succubi. The following is one of the numerous old tales of this type: "In Nantes [France] there lived a certain unfortunate woman who was pursued by a brazen devil. He appeared to her in the guise of a beautiful spirit. Concealing his evil designs, he succeeded through guile and flattery in persuading the soul of the unfortunate one to look favorably on his passion. Upon receiving her consent, he took the feet of the unfortunate one in one hand, and put his other hand on her head, the symbols of intimacy by which he wedded her, so to speak. The unfortunate woman's husband, a fine nobleman, had no suspicion of this guilty union. Ever an invisible lover, the foul one kept up these relations...and wore her out with his incredible debauchery."[25]

Today comparable instances of this belief are extremely rare, and in them the role of the demon is taken over by the hallucinatory image of a dead husband or lover. In the twenties I knew a young woman, a nearly illiterate houseworker, blooming with health, who confessed to me that her husband, who was killed in the war, came to her every night, that she saw him, touched him, and "continued to live with him as husband

---

[24] A. Lehmann, op. cit., p. 507.
[25] M. Simon, *Mir gryoz* (The Word of Dreams), St. Petersburg, 1890, p. 63.

and wife." Such hallucinations, colored by strong sexual urges, were frequent in convents and monasteries, and they, too, sustained the belief in the posthumous existence of the individual person.

The French psychiatrist, Simon, distinguishes a separate category which he calls "physiological hallucinations," manifested by healthy, even eminent, people. In describing the battle of Austerlitz, Balzac heard the cries of the wounded, the roar of cannons, the salvos of guns; when Flaubert wrote the poisoning scene in *Madame Bovary,* the taste of arsenic in his mouth was so real that he retched. Goethe was also subjected to hallucinations; once in broad daylight he saw himself in his usual attire and on horseback. Goethe could evoke any visual hallucinatory image at will, which later, this time involuntarily, were transformed into other images. This astonishing faculty is sometimes encountered even among "plain mortals." In her youth, my mother, too, possessed the ability to evoke hallucinatory images. In the summertime she would lie on her back on the ground and, with eyes screwed up, gaze at the sky; gradually panoramas of strange lands, cities, castles and cottages, groups of people, and at times entire scenes became clearly outlined on this background — fragmentary reflections, evidently, of what she had at one time or another read or seen in books.

The First International Congress on Experimental Psychology, held in Paris in 1899, circulated a large number of questionnaires designed to obtain accurate data on the importance of hallucinations in the genesis of various kinds of superstition. Over 27,000 answers were received. More than

3,000 of these answers (approximately 12 per cent) were affirmative, that is, they informed the Congress that the recipient of the questionnaire, once, or more than once, had had hallucinations while in a normal state of health. In the majority of cases the hallucinations were visual. Auditory hallucinations were more rare, and tactile hallucinations still rarer. Half of the auditory hallucinations consisted in people hearing their name called. This species of hallucinations has given rise to one of the folk superstitions: whoever thinks he hears his name called, especially if it happens in the spring ("the voices of spring"), let him expect quick death.

In origin, hallucinations are allied to dreams. They are a kind of dream while awake. The twilight state of consciousness which we experience just before falling asleep, or immediately after awakening, promotes the appearance of so-called hypnagogic hallucinations. If during the day we have been long and enthusiastically gathering mushrooms, or fishing, then often, just before falling asleep, we vividly see large clusters of these mushrooms, or fish wriggling in the air. During such a state of "pre-sleep," even perfectly healthy people may have genuine, at times frightening, hallucinations.

There are known cases of the spontaneous transition of dreams into hallucinations. Thus, Liébeault relates that once, when he dreamt of a fire, he continued to see this fire after he woke up. "When one dreams that he is being shot at by a pistol," writes Simon, "there is much ground for expecting that this dream will be followed by prompt awakening. The subjective sensation is at times so intense that the sound still rings in the ears of the awakened person — he continues to hear it."[26]

All this shows that the hallucinations which lead to such fear in superstitious people are no more mysterious than dreams, and that, like dreams, they may be caused by various artificial methods. Many ways of telling fortunes are based on these methods, already known to the peoples of antiquity. Thus, visual hallucinations were evoked when a fortune teller gazed persistently into a crystal ball (crystallomancy) or at a "magic fluid" — water (hydromancy), later replaced by a mirror; listening to the murmur of seashells aroused auditory hallucinations, and so forth. It is obvious that by use of these methods the fortune teller puts himself into a light hypnotic state, heightening suggestibility and, consequently, proneness to hallucinations. Unbelievably vivid and heterogeneous hallucinatory images may be evoked by the use of poisonous substances — hashish, opium, mescaline, and others. The "Sabbath flight" of the Middle Ages is also a concatenation of visual hallucinations, caused by rubbing the skin with a mixture of poisonous substances — the "witches' salves."

To this day the practice of drinking the juice of a local cactus plant, called peyotl (Echinocactus Williamsii), is maintained among the Mexican Indians. This juice allegedly awakens the gift of prophecy and clairvoyance. In 1925 the French pharmacologist, Rouhier, brought the cactus to Europe. When he tried it on himself and other Europeans, there was observed unusually intense and prolonged excitation of the visual area of the cerebral cortex; when the eyes were shut, a

---

[26] Ibid., p. 6.

kaleidoscope of extremely vivid and beautiful images, yielding esthetic delight, arose spontaneously in the field of vision. This phenomenon is occasioned by the presence of mescaline in the extract of the aforementioned cactus. There are also present in peyotl other alkaloids, whose action leads to collateral psycho-physiological disturbances.

We had the opportunity to conduct several experiments concerning the effects produced by the extract of peyotl on two healthy subjects, female students twenty and twenty-four years of age. Following the intake of the peyotl extract, they experienced a sharp intensification of auditory as well as visual sensations and perceptions: the objects around them seemed to be more vividly colored, the sounds more resonant. When they shut their eyes, visual imagery of objects perceived was retained for a long time, and seemed no less real than the objects themselves. At the same time, the rare phenomenon of synesthesia was also observed: chords in various keys that were struck on the piano seemed deafening, and, on closing the eyes, evoked every time the sensation of a flash of light, colored in one or another hue.

With progressive intoxication, motor and emotional excitation increased. Though consciousness was retained all the time, it was powerless to stop the stream of words and movements. The will was paralyzed and unable to suppress sudden emotional outbursts. According to the subjects' own account, they felt very gay, everything seemed to them to be extremely beautiful, and "you could get away with anything." Time seemed to fly with incredible swiftness, and for this reason the actions and speech of people around one seemed irritatingly slow. The mind worked feverishly, making sudden leaps and turns. The handwriting changed radically: it became larger and bolder.

Above all, one should note the sharp heightening of suggestibility to a degree characteristic of the hypnotic state. Experiments on "mind reading" (see Chapter V) during the period of peyotl intoxication worked incomparably more quickly and more accurately than in the usual state. This indicates intensification of the capacity for motor automatism in the subjects.[27]

But let us return to modern hypnotic experiments. It is possible to effect by means of suggestion various changes in the character traits and behavior of the person under hypnosis comparable to those that develop spontaneously in some hysterics. It is possible during a séance to instill in a man with somnambulistic tendencies the conviction that he is not at all just humble Ivan Ivanovich but some historic figure, whereupon the somnambulist will begin to impersonate this famous person, often with amazing skill and realism. Some somnambulists during hypnotic sleep undergo radical personality changes independently of the hypnotist's suggestions. A placid, silent man becomes irritable, restless, and garrulous. He remembers nothing of his life, but instead clearly recalls everything that happened during previous hypnotic séances or what had been seen in his nocturnal dreams. This is a disturbing symptom,

---

[27] See L. L. Vasiliev, E. T. Galvas, Ya. I. Perikhanyats, and P. V. Terentiev, "K voprosu o psikhofiziologicheskam deystvii peotla." (On the Question of the Psychophysiological Effect of Peyotl), in *Trudy Instituta mozga,* XVII (Leningrad, 1947), p. 55.

pointing to a pathological form of hypnosis in the given subject, a tendency toward "split personality" — a condition which, as we have seen in the cases of the hysteric, Felida, and the young man described by the French psychologist, Binet, may gradually develop to a surprising degree.

In the case of the young male patient, Binet was able, through hypnotic suggestion, to summon forth artificially the traits of one personality or the other. When it was suggested to the patient that he was working in the vineyard, he, on awaking, behaved as if he really were working there; he was unable to sew a stitch, and his legs functioned normally. At the next séance it was suggested to him that he was a nine- or ten-year-old boy; on awaking, he behaved as if he really were such a boy, he was convinced that he was working in a tailoring shop and that his legs were paralyzed; and while in this condition he was, in fact, unable to walk, but could sew skillfully. Thus, the hypnosis evoked that which in life had been brought about by catastrophic shocks to the nervous system. Together with this, in hypnosis, traits characteristic of one personality gave way swiftly and directly to traits characteristic of the other. "The impression is created," wrote N. E. Vvedensky on this matter, "that the different periods of life put away, so to speak, their impressions in the brain in layers, and that these layers of impressions and traces of former experiences may [under the influence of hypnotic suggestion] retreat from the active state and again re-emerge into it, each by itself alone."[28]

The suggestibility of some hypnotics of the somnambu-

---

[28] *Polnoe sobranie sochineniy*, V, p. 355.

listic type is so great that verbal suggestion begins to affect even such purely physiological processes as, it would seem, cannot possibly have any connection with the mind. The following are several remarkable facts, established by Professor K. I. Platonov and other authorities in the field of hypnosis.[29]

The suggestion of satiety ("mock feeding") brings on increase in the number of leucocytes in the blood — the so-called digestive leucocytosis, usually observed after actual consumption of food. Conversely, the suggestion of hunger leads, as does actual hunger, to leucopenia, that is, to decrease of the leucocytic content in the blood. Greater intake of sugar causes some increase of glucose in the blood even in healthy people; an analogous phenomenon takes place during suggested (mock) feeding with sugar. If it is suggested to a hypnotic that he is very thirsty and that he is drinking glass after glass of water, increased secretion of urine with lowered specific gravity will begin quickly; that is, the same thing will take place as that following the actual intake of large quantities of water into the organism. The suggested sensation of cold brings on paling of the skin, shivering, and "goose flesh"; and, as happens when one is really cold, there is a considerable increase (30 or more per cent) in the respiratory exchange of gases; that is, in the quantity of absorbed oxygen and secreted carbon dioxide.

Similarly, some authors point out that it is also possible to increase bodily temperature by suggesting chills and heat — "mock fever."

[29] K. I. Platonov, *Slovo kak fiziologicheski i lechebni faktor*, 3rd ed., Moscow, 1962. (English tr.: The Word as a Physiological and Therapeutic Factor, tr. from 2nd Russian ed. by David A. Myshne. Moscow: Foreign Languages Publishing House, 1959.)

Finally, experiments, about which there is no longer any doubt, with "mock burns" and "mock blows" are especially instructive, though these experiments succeed only with those rare somnambulists who manifest an exceptionally high degree of suggestibility. If one touches a specific area of the skin with a wooden stick and at the same time suggests that this area is being seared with a red-hot iron, an actual burn — reddened skin, a blister, and so forth — will eventually appear at the part burned in mock fashion. The touch of a pencil, accompanied by the suggestion that it is a powerful blow, leads to the appearance of a blue mark — a bruise — on the spot touched.

All these experiments — at first sight incredible — are possible because every internal organ, every blood vessel, every section of the dermal covering is connected with the "psychic organ"— the cerebral cortex — by means of neural conductors through the spinal cord and subcortical formations. As a result, those specific physiological processes which operate in the cortex and which underlie various psychic states may, under certain conditions, interfere with the functions of different organs, altering their activity. Such interference operates, apparently, in the category of conditioned-reflex formation. The following interesting observation of the noted hypnologist, P. P. Podyapolsky, speaks for this: the power of suggestion can provoke a burn only in those subjects who had suffered at least one actual burn caused by contact with some hot object.

Dr. Podyapolsky confirmed this important observation by the following experiment: "Once," he writes, "I tried unsuccessfully to induce in a peasant a reddening of the skin from a mock mustard plaster; not only was there no reddening, there wasn't even any appropriate sensation of burning or smarting. I surmised that this simple man had probably never experienced a mustard plaster; therefore, his mind lacked the corresponding images and the ability to reproduce them with all their consequences...And so it turned out—he had never experienced a mustard plaster. It happened that he later had occasion to put a mustard plaster on his chest, and when I hypnotized him thereafter, suggestion quickly created not only the appropriate burning sensation but also reddening of the skin where the mock mustard plaster was applied."[30]

The principle of the dominant (from the Latin verb *dominare* — to rule), which was proposed by A. A. Ukhtomsky as early as 1923, plays a great role in the phenomena of hypnosis and suggestion along with the mechanisms of conditioned reflexes. A dominant is a locus of heightened excitability and steady excitation, temporarily prevailing in the central nervous system and arising under defined conditions in some division of the brain or spinal cord. The locus as dominant prevails, first of all, by, so to speak, attracting to itself excitatory impulses from other simultaneously active nerve centers, summating these within itself and thereby intensifying itself. Secondly, the dominance of such a locus of excitation consists in inhibiting both those nerve centers that do not contribute to it and their corresponding reflexes. Thanks to these two properties, the dominant, while it obtains, transforms and directs all nervous activity its way. For instance: the alimentary

---

[30] P. P. Podyapolsky, *Voldyr ot mnimovo ozhoga, prichinenniy slovesnym vnusheniem* (A Blister from a Mock Burn, Caused by Verbal Suggestion), Saratov, 1905, p. 12.

dominant, created by persistent impulses from an empty stomach and intestines, directs the entire behavior of the hungry being, man or animal, toward the finding and taking of food. The sexual dominant functions in its behalf, as does the defense dominant, which is linked to the feeling of fear. Dominants of lower order constitute the neural foundation of instincts, which, like their basis — the dominants — have a short-range character, one superseding the other. Dominants of higher order, formed in the cerebral cortex, constitute the physiological basis of certain psychic faculties, among them such important ones as attention, ability to concentrate, and memory. "The act of attention must harbor some steady locus of excitation along with inhibition of other centers,"[31] wrote Ukhtomsky, pointing out that a foremost psychoneurologist, V. M. Bekhterev, agrees with this thesis.

According to Bekhterev, the principal feature of hypnotism consists in its suppression of the hypnotic's independent activity: a hypnotized person loses his ability to concentrate his attention on anything in the world around him and for this reason does not take active or personal notice of the influences from the outside on his sensory organs. It is understandable that in this helpless state the hypnotic should fall into the power of the hypnotist: having lost his independence and freedom of action, the hypnotic's attention can be directed to any given object only through the suggesting command of the hypnotist. Translating this psychological conception of hyp-

---

[31] For a more detailed account, see L. L. Vasiliev, *Printsip dominanty v psikhologii* (The Principle of the Dominant in Psychology), *Vestnik Leningradskovo universiteta*, No. 9 (1950), p. 32.

nosis into the language of the theory of the dominant, Bekhterev gives the following physiological explanation of the basic hypnotic phenomena:

"Active concentration, by being a so-called dominant in the physiological sense; that is, the expressor of intensified excitation of centers in the prefrontal areas, suppresses by this very fact the activity of all other cortical areas receiving impulses from the external world. Conversely, with suppression of active concentration, functioning as a dominant, every direction of concentration, by means of verbal influence (suggestion), toward any perceiving apparatus of the cerebral cortex — whether visual, auditory, or tactile-muscular — creates in this instance conditions for the appearance of a dominant in the corresponding cortical center, and this intensifies the latter's activity to such a degree that hallucinatory images emerge with vividness in some cases, or, in others, an action that was suggested takes place.

"On the other hand, inhibition of concentration with reference to a given external stimulus evokes the phenomena we know by the name of "negative hallucinations"— a condition during which the hypnotic does not see [even with his eyes open], does not hear, and does not feel the objects around him. If one bears in mind that, with suppression of active concentration, the direction of the hypnotic is in the hands of the hypnotist, it is not difficult to account for the appearance of rapport between the hypnotic and hypnotist, since concentration in the hypnotic is directed solely by the speech of the hypnotist, serving as special stimulus, nor can it be directed by the speech of anyone else without special suggestion on the part of the hypnotist.

"As for posthypnotic amnesia [failure to remember anything that occurred during hypnosis], it is an inevitable consequence of the fact that, as happens also during the waking state, we reproduce [recall] out of our past only that to which our active concentration, which is just what is suppressed under hypnosis, was directed at the time. All the rest cannot be reproduced until it leads to a combined [conditioned-reflex] connection with active concentration."[32]

Bekhterev's views of the physiological nature of hypnosis do not contradict Pavlov's view of hypnosis as partial sleep — incomplete inhibition of the cortex with preservation in it of "sentry points" of highly graphic excitation, maintained by the verbal stimuli proceeding from the hypnotist. It may be said that these "sentry points" of excitation constitute the dominant, brought about in the cortex by the hypnotist, directed toward him, and inseparably connected with him.

---

[32] V. M. Bekhterev, "Priroda gipnoza," (The Nature of Hypnosis), *Vestnik znania,* No. 1 (1926), pp. 38-39.

CHAPTER IV

Suggestion and Autosuggestion During the Waking State

CHAPTER IV

Suggestion and Autosuggestion During the Waking State

TODAY THE NERVOUS MECHANISM behind the phenomena of suggestion and autosuggestion has been fully revealed by natural science. In the past these phenomena were taken for miracles. It has long been known that bleeding sores, so-called "stigmata," have appeared on the hands and feet of people who gave themselves up to religious ecstasy and keenly imagined to themselves Christ's sufferings on the Cross, and that these "stigmata" appeared in places corresponding to the wounds of the crucified Christ. In his lectures N. E. Vvedensky reports such a case which took place somewhat recently (in the 19th century—involving a peasant girl named Lateaux. "The Belgian Academy of Sciences organized a special commission to investigate this case. One of the young girl's hands was carefully bandaged, even sealed; on Good Friday, at the hour of Christ's Passion on the Cross, the seals were broken and the bandage removed. On the hand that was sealed there were localized bruises. Thus," Vvedensky concludes, "it is possible by a certain kind of autosuggestion to exert localized influences on both the vasomotor system and the autonomic [trophic] processes even during the waking state [and not only during hypnosis]."[1]

It is now and then possible to notice similar phenomena in weakly expressed form in everyday life. To illustrate, I cite the following incident, witnessed with my own eyes and recorded then and there by me. On emerging from a very hot rural bathhouse, an acquaintance of mine, a young man, noticed a disgusting kind of insect, an earwig, which he had never encountered before. With a feeling of disgust he picked it up with the fingers of his right hand in order to examine it more closely. The earwig arched and tried, with its "pincers," to pinch the finger holding it, but failed, for, with a surprised shriek, the young man shook it off to the ground with a sharp movement of the hand. Nonetheless, distinct crimson marks were soon visible on the skin of the fingers that had held the insect, one on the thumb and two on the index finger. There was no smarting, no sensation of pain in the reddened places of the skin; but it was impossible to wash away the marks. Without doubt they were manifestations of a local dilation of the cutaneous blood vessels brought on by the auto-suggested thought of an imaginary bite and by fright experienced in connection with it. It is possible that his preceding stay in the bathhouse, with its sharp alternating action of hot and cold water on the skin, had intensified the reactiveness of the reflex vasomotor apparatus, and thereby promoted the emergence of the phenomenon described.

---

[1] N. E. Vvedensky, *Polnoe sobranie sochineniy* (Collected Works), p. 349.

When religious superstitions were widespread, the phenomena of mutual suggestion and autosuggestion during the waking state would sometimes grip a great number of people at one time; the phenomena took on, so to speak, an infectious character and grew into so-called psychic epidemics. In one of his books V. M. Bekhterev[2] described the various forms of psychic epidemics that arose at various times in different countries — such as, for instance, collective hallucinations, mass attacks of hysteroid convulsions, epidemic belief in being possessed by the devil or bewitched, and so on.

"To cure possession by the devil, the plague, and hysterics," he wrote, "people usually resorted to religious usages, namely: freeing such 'possessed' people of the devil by means of prayer, or pronouncing incantations against the devil in church — to bow to God and leave the 'possessed one' — which usually resulted in either a stream of even rougher blasphemous words and gestures or a new attack of convulsions. If we were to visit a modern psychiatric clinic, we would find there patients in the category of hysteria or suffering from hysteroepilepsy. The pathological symptoms are similar to the symptoms described in people 'possessed by the devil,' with only this difference: the devil no longer figures in the gibberish of the patient. However, we see in these patients the same typical 'arch' when an hysterical woman arches herself bowlike, with only her heels and top of her head touching the bed, and the same contraction of the upper and lower extremities.

"In the past such cases were cured by the power of sug-

---

[2] *Vnushenie i evo rol v obshchestvennoy zhizni* (Suggestion and Its Role in Social Life), St. Petersburg, 1908.

gestion [applied in the waking state] in association with religious enthusiasm. At the present time patients likewise yield to treatment by suggestion, conducted by a doctor capable of instilling faith in a future cure. In just the same way at the beginning of our era, the 'one-armed,' the 'enfeebled,' and the 'seeming dead' were cured. There is complete basis for affirming that in ancient times the general designation of 'one-armed' and 'enfeebled' encompassed all paralytics, including those stricken with hysterical paralysis of the arms or legs — people who, as is known, are generally susceptible to therapeutic suggestion."[3]

Though it seems unbelievable, similar psychic epidemics may be observed even today. Scattered instances occurred during the war. The temporary occupation of part of Soviet territory by the German fascist aggressors engendered conditions for a certain revival and spread of bourgeois ideology, religious and other superstitions. The burdens of war, the death of many people, anxiety about one's personal fate and the fate of one's kin, and uncertainty about the next day promoted this phenomenon not a little. The following instance, which occurred in Yelabug in the winter of 1943 and was recorded by me at that time, is a case in point.

Two local residents, female students at a factory school, twenty-year-old P. and sixteen-year-old Z., first one, then the other, received "anonymous letters" in which there was scrawled that, for such and such an action, on such a day and hour, they would be punished with illness — writhing, loss

[3] V. M. Bekhterev, "Vnushenie i chudesnye istselenia" (Suggestion and Miraculous Cures), *Vestnik znania,* No. 5 (1925), p. 324.

of voice and speech, deafness, pains in the head and arms...
At the indicated times all this was fulfilled in full measure.
P. was afflicted for three weeks with the symptoms of illness
suggested by the letter, Z., for several days. Both girls later
related that an old woman appeared to them in a dream and
allegedly put a "curse" on them. A medical assistant from the
local polyclinic was called in to attend the sick girls, and the
"anonymous letters" were turned over to a people's court,
which interrogated witnesses. It remains to be added that
several girls, who visited the patients and witnessed their convulsions, showed the same hysterical symptoms in weakened
form. This was nothing but the beginning of a real psychic
epidemic which was fortunately extinguished in short order.

Instances of individual autosuggestion, leading to various
kinds of "psychogenic illness," are encountered more often.
An obsession in the mind of a hypochondriac that an organ,
which is in reality perfectly healthy, is diseased, may lead to
actual disturbance of the functional performance of the organ.
This may happen not only with uneducated, but also with
educated people, and even doctors.

The Academician I. P. Tarkhanov cites an interesting
case in point. "A well-known doctor, in the course of lecturing
on cardio-vascular diseases, began to pay too much attention
to the functioning of his own heart; very heavy pounding of
the heart appeared and his pulse became irregular. He was
delivered from this self-induced illness only through a trip
undertaken for the purpose of distracting his attention from
the pathological sensations in the region of his heart."[4]

---

[4] I. P. Tarkhanov, "Dukh i telo" (Spirit and Body), *Vestnik i biblioteka samoobrazovania,* Supplement, p. 160.

The case of Dr. Eisemann, who treated Princess Schwarzenberg, is even more amusing. On his first visit to his distinguished patient he was greatly embarrassed by loud intestinal rumblings caused by increased peristalsis. Consequently, during later visits he greatly feared the repetition of these sounds. But he had only to approach the patient's bed to evoke loud rumbling in his abdomen. This happened every day for a whole week, though during visits to other patients his intestines were in complete quiet. Reduced to despair, Eisemann finally decided to address the princess as follows: "Your Highness," he said, "for a whole week you've been hearing intestinal rumblings which are an extreme embarrassment to me. On my first visit the rumblings were an accident; their subsequent repetition was, however, occasioned precisely by my fear of such repetition and my thinking about it. To put an end to the matter, I decided to explain it to you and to ask your pardon." Remarkably, following this explanation, there were no more intestinal rumblings during visits to this particular patient.[5]

It is not surprising that reverse instances are also possible; in which truly disturbed organic functions may be restored to normalcy through appropriate suggestion or autosuggestion. This is the basis of psychotherapeutic methods which, in the hands of doctors who skilfully apply suggestion and autosuggestion, frequently effect remarkable results in the treatment of illnesses caused by disturbances of nervous and neuropsychic activity.

---

[5] Ibid., p. 155.

Today treatment by suggestion in hypnosis or in the waking state rests on a solid foundation — I. P. Pavlov's theory of higher nervous activity. Psychotherapists apply suggestion with full understanding of why it works and which nervous mechanisms are set in operation therewith. In the past the therapeutic power of verbal suggestion was used blindly, without understanding what it was really all about, and for this reason it frequently brought more harm than good to the patient. The magic exorcisms of a magician, the incantations of a sorcerer were, in essence, a naive form of verbal suggestion, based on superstitious ideas, which, nevertheless, sometimes achieved their ends. This the ignorant took for "miraculous healing."

The following is an example of such suggestive incantational exorcism of various ills with water: "Salt — salt everything! Ashes — corrode everything! Black coal — blacken everything! Salt everything, salt; corrode, ashes; blacken, black coal! Whosoever drinks of this water — from him all ailments shall fall away! Whosoever licks these ashes—from him all sicknesses shall flee! Whosoever tastes of the salt — from him all illnesses shall be driven! Whosoever bites of the coal — blinded shall be his eyes! Such and such a sick one drinks the water. My true word has been fulfilled — true as true can be!"[6]

"The secret of therapeutic suggestion," wrote Bekhterev in this connection, "was known to many common folk, who for centuries transmitted this secret by word of mouth in the guise of magic, sorcery, witchcraft, and so forth ... Autosuggestion frequently functions side by side with suggestion, when a person himself believes in the miraculous power of some remedy."

Thus, autosuggestion explains, for example, the action of many so-called "sympathetic" remedies, which frequently exhibit a therapeutic effect. Ferraus cured fever with the aid of a piece of paper on which two words were scrawled: "Against fever," and each day the patient had to tear off one letter. There are known instances of cures effected by "bread pills," "water from the Neva," a simple "laying on of hands," and so on. And all this is explained by the fact that in some people, due to their unusual suggestibility, it is possible, by word alone and with sufficiently suggestive intonation, to effect all those transformations — in the paralyzed, the lame, the convulsives, and the mad — which, prompted by widespread belief in demonic powers, occurred so frequently in ancient and, especially, medieval times. Therefore, it is easy to heal suggestible people by these and other means, regardless of seemingly essential differences among them.[7]

Let us adduce yet another curious example. Since ancient times various popular "sympathetic" remedies have been applied for the removal of warts. All of them are calculated to have as great an effect as possible on the patient's imagination and in this way to suggest to him a faith in their therapeutic power. Doctors have "scientized" this age-old procedure for curing warts and are today applying it successfully. In his article, "On the Treatment of Warts by Hypnosis," Bruno Bloch gives the following results he achieved. Fifty-five (30.7%)

---

[6] See F. F. Fisher, *Lechenie magicheskimi, okkulticheskimi i simpaticheskimi sredstvami* (Healing by Magical, Occult, and Sympathetic Remedies), St. Petersburg, 1908, p. 47.

[7] V. M. Bekhterev, "Vnushenie i chudesniye istselenia," (Suggestion and Miraculous Cures) *vestnik znania,* No. 5 (1925), p. 327.

out of 179 patients were cured in one hypnotic session, thirty-two (17.9%) in two sessions, eight (4.4%) in three sessions, three (1.7%) in several sessions. Altogether, ninety-eight (54.7%) patients were cured. Two (1.1%) were cured only partially, and seventy-nine (44.2%) were not cured. In this way, over half the patients were rid of their warts.[8] The success of such treatments depends first of all on both the degree of suggestibility in the patient and on the type of wart ("flat," "common," etc.). Heightening of suggestibility was attained by inducing hypnotic sleep, but cures were gotten in those who were the most suggestible even without hypnosis — in the waking state.

Cures for various ailments were sometimes effected in those who were fervent believers in the miraculous power of ikons and relics; but they were brought about by powerfully acting autosuggestion. Needless to say, such results are obtainable only when the illness itself is of a psychogenic nature; that is, it has been produced by some mental shock and has consisted of a reversible functional disturbance of the normal activity of the nervous system (without structural damage). Examples of such illnesses are: the paralyses, the loss of cutaneous sensitivity, blindness and muteness of hysterics — in brief, those ailments which are today the most responsive to the therapeutic suggestions of psychotherapists. Below are some instances from V. M. Bekhterev's medical practice:

For the purpose of demonstration, a patient who had spent

---

[8] See A. I. Kartamyshev, *Gipnoz i vnushenie v terapii kozhnykh bolezney* (The Therapeutic Use of Hypnosis and Suggestion in Skin Diseases), Moscow, 1953.

a month and a half in the clinic was wheeled into the auditorium where Bekhterev was lecturing to his medical students. The patient had suffered a sudden paralysis following an hysterical attack, and as a result had been unable to move his legs for over nine months. In the school auditorium he was hypnotized: then, by means of suggestion, he was raised to his feet, taken around the room, at the same time being told that he was no longer a paralytic, and that he would walk after awaking. When he was brought out of the hypnotic state, the "paralytic," to the astonishment of the audience and to his own delight, walked unaided to the hospital ward — a feat that amazed the clinical section. Then, while in the waking state, it was suggested to the patient that his convulsive hysterical attacks would cease — whereupon he became once and for all freed of them.

Another example. A sick peasant woman for a long time had contracture of the arm, which the usual medical treatment had failed to cure. Bekhterev corrected her arm while she was under hypnosis. On awaking, the "one-armed" peasant woman showed her arm, which she raised above her head, to the audience with irrepressible exclamations of joy: "It's well! Look, look, it's all well!" But it is the cure of hereditary blindness by hypnotic suggestion that Bekhterev himself considers to be his most remarkable case. This case astonished even experienced eye specialists, who had considered it to be a type of blindness incurable by any medical means.[9]

Numerous, apparently trustworthy, accounts of fakirs,

---

[9] V. M. Bekhterev, "Vnushenie i chudesniye istselenia" (Suggestion and Miraculous Cures), *Vestnik znania*, No. 5 (1925), p. 329.

religious fanatics, medieval witches and sorcerers attest to the fact that in the state of ecstasy they lost all sensitivity to pain and endured, with amazing fortitude, the most incredible self-tortures, torments and the like. It is quite possible that in these cases, too, a certain degree of autohypnosis, the suggestive action of fanatical faith or autosuggestion, played some kind of role.

From time to time there appear in European circuses individuals who demonstrate their insensitivity to pain. I once met such a person, a man bearing the sonorous Indian name of To-Rama but actually an Austrian by birth. He was a chemical engineer, but also specialized in hypnotizing various wild animals. He was devoted to his work and was a trustworthy man. From his own lips I learned the story (later published in the press)[10] of how he cultivated the ability to inhibit and deaden sensitivity to pain. Puncturing his palms, shoulders, back, etc. with a thick, long needle did indeed fail to produce any objective indices of sensed pain: his pulse and his blood pressure registered no changes at the time of puncture; reflex pupillary contraction — a reliable index of concealed pain — was also not observed.

To-Rama's story told how, toward the end of the first World War, he was gravely wounded by a splinter from an explosive. At the field hospital his condition was pronounced hopeless — he overheard the doctors discussing it — and he was transferred to the ward for the mortally wounded. "Then

---

[10] See *Chto pishut o To-Rama: otzyvy russkoy i inostrannoy pechati* (Reports about To-Rama — Excerpts from the Russian and Foreign Press), Leningrad gostsirk, 1926.

something in me rebelled," To-Rama wrote. "I gritted my teeth, and I had only one thought: 'You must stay alive, you won't die, you feel no pain.' *I repeated this endlessly,* until this thought penetrated my flesh and blood to such an extent that finally I ceased to feel any pain. I don't know how, but the incredible did happen. The doctors shook their heads. From day to day my condition improved. Thus, by will power alone, I stayed alive. Two months later I underwent minor surgery in a Viennese hospital without any general, or even local anesthetic; autosuggestion alone sufficed. After I had completely recovered, I developed my system of victory over the self in this connection to so high a degree that I feel no pain when I do not wish to feel it."

What To-Rama was able to achieve through autosuggestion, psychotherapists achieve by suggestion under hypnosis, or even in the waking state. In those cases where the state of health contra-indicates anesthesia, it is possible, if the patient is sufficiently suggestible, to perform surgery on him under hypnosis or even in the waking, posthypnotic state, after suggestion, directed toward elimination or prevention of pain, had been made in hypnosis. Painless childbirth is achieved in the same way.

All this demonstrates that one can inhibit selectively, by means of verbal suggestion, or through autosuggestion, those reflex centers of the brain that control the sensations of pain. But it is also possible, by the application of the same methods of suggestion and autosuggestion, to create and maintain in the central nervous system one or another locus of prolonged, steady excitation and heightened excitability; that is, the same thing which A. A. Ukhtomsky called the dominant.

In the story cited above, To-Rama calls special attention to the fact that he achieved his aim by repeating the same thought, the same sentence, "endlessly." It is just this tireless repetition of the very same thing which constitutes the principal condition for the formation of the dominant, and is the secret of the beneficial action of autosuggestion—a secret which was known from ancient times to the Eastern peoples and to Christian zealots, and which is applied by psychotherapists in a theoretically anchored and "scientized" form.

Indian and Tibetan Buddhists attain a state of ecstasy through incessant reiteration of prayer appealing to the Buddha: "Om, mani pad-me khum!" ("Hail, Precious Stone in the lotus blossom!" "Precious Stone" is one of the Buddha's common names). In order not to trouble themselves with the endless utterance of these words, the Buddhists use a so-called "prayer wheel,"—a rotating drum on which the above words are inscribed. Revolving the drum in front of him, the Buddhist rhythmically reads through the prayer a countless number of times.

Among the Christian zealots the same role was played by a similarly brief "Jesus-prayer." "Take a rosary," directs an old precept, "according to which you recite the prayer at least three thousand times a day at first [afterwards the daily repititions of this prayer were gradually increased to twelve thousand]. Sit silent and alone, bow your head, close your eyes, breathe quietly, look with your mind's eye into your heart, put your mind [that is, thought] from your head into your heart. With your breathing, recite: 'Lord Jesus Christ, have mercy on me' [this is the 'Jesus-prayer'] — quietly, with your lips or only in your mind. Try to banish thought, have quiet patience, and repeat your exercise more frequently."

In a rare old book, *A Pilgrim's Frank Story to His Spiritual Father*,[11] there is a remarkable account of the manner in which a certain pilgrim learned to "pray incessantly" and the state of blissful ecstasy into which he was thereby absorbed. One cannot refrain from citing at least a brief excerpt from this book.

"And thus, I still wander today, and ceaselessly recite the Jesus-prayer, which is sweeter and more precious to me than anything in the world. I sometimes walk seventy or more versts[12] a day, unaware that I am walking, aware only that I am reciting a prayer. When severe cold grips me, I begin to pray more vigorously and soon feel warm all over. When hunger begins to overcome me, I invoke the name of Jesus Christ more often, and forget that I want to eat. When I get sick and rheumatic pains begin in my back and legs, I begin to attend to the prayer and do not feel the pain. When I am abused, I need only to recall how sweet is the Jesus-prayer and then and there abuse and anger go away and I forget everything. I have become a little half-witted, have no cares, and nothing interests me. I would rather not look on anything earthly and would rather be always alone. I want only, as is my wont, forever to repeat my prayer; and when I am engaged in this,

---

[11] *Otkrovenniy rasskaz strannika dukhovnomu svoyemu otsu*, Kazan, 1881.

[12] Approximately 47 miles — Tr.

I feel very joyous. God knows what is the matter with me."

Let us now see into what prosaic form this method of frequently repeated autosuggestion has been transformed in contemporary psychotherapy. According to Bekhterev, a definite autosuggestive formula should be worked out for every separate case. This formula should be appropriate to the given case and be spoken by the patient himself affirmatively and in the present, not the future, tense. Let us assume, for instance, that a man, addicted to wine-drinking, should want to cure himself of his addiction by means of autosuggestion. He must utter the autosuggestive formula in the following form: "I have taken a pledge, not only not to drink, but not even to think of wine; now I have completely freed myself of this ruinous temptation, and never think of it." He has to repeat such a verbal autosuggestive formula *many times,* in a low voice, preferably before sleep and in the morning, immediately after waking, and then *with full concentration.* If only there is concentration on it, such autosuggestion can be effective in a number of cases.[13]

The greatest success in the therapeutic application of autosuggestion in the recent past fell to the lot of a certain Emile Coué, who was not even a doctor but just a druggist in the French city of Nantes, an old scientific center of hypnology. Coué's method spread far and wide and acquired fervent adherents all over the world. This method, like that of Bekhterev's just described, consists of prolonged whispering of a verbal autosuggestive formula, composed in affirmative

---

[13] V. M. Bekhterev, *Gipnosis, vnushenie i psikhoterapia,* (Hypnosis, Suggestion, and Psychotherapy), St. Petersburg, 1911, p. 53.

and categorical expressions and appropriate for the given case. There is, however, a basic difference: Coué's method, unlike Bekhterev's, does not require that the whispering be done with "full concentration;" instead, it should be done automatically, in a patter, in a state of complete passivity and so-called mental vacuum (as much as possible, there should be no thinking about anything whatsoever during the time of autosuggestion).

Strange as Coué's method may seem at first glance, it nonetheless had an undoubted therapeutic effect in a number of cases. Like verbal suggestion in hypnosis (see the end of the previous chapter), it is based on the same nervous mechanism of formation in the central nervous system — in this case in the cerebral cortex — of a powerful, long acting dominant, capable of effecting reorganizations in the organism and the psyche — reorganizations corresponding to its character. In the formation of such a dominant the ecstatic states of the Buddhists and Christian zealots, described in this chapter, find their explanation. I know also that A. A. Ukhtomsky held such an opinion about this matter.

CHAPTER V

Automatic
Movements

CHAPTER V

Automatic Movements

IN 1848, THERE TOOK PLACE an event, involving the Fox family in America, which was fated to become the start of the most astonishing psychic epidemic of modern times, explainable by the progressive crisis of capitalist society, by the predictable growth in it of mysticism, and all kinds of superstitions.

The city of Rochester, in which this family lived, became the birthplace of spiritism — a superstition that quickly spread throughout America, then jumped to Europe. The phenomenon, which engendered the enthusiasm of spiritism, consisted of the following: when members of the Fox family — father, mother, and three young daughters — sat around a table and placed their hands on it, the table moved, rocked from side to side, and began to emit crackling and tapping sounds. And, if the participants in the séance recited the alphabet, words and whole sentences were composed of those letters whose enunciation coincided with the tappings: these were accepted as messages from the "other world" by the superstitious participants of like séances. The news spread that, owing to the miraculous abilities of the Fox girls to serve as intermediaries — mediums — between the world of the dead and that of the living, it had become possible for the souls of the dead (they began to be called "spirits") at long last to communicate with the living. It soon developed, however, that "mediumistic abilities" were not so rare. Mediums sprang up everywhere, "table turning" became the fashion, fascinating first hundreds, then thousands and hundreds of thousands. Even scientists of world renown were carried away by this novel form of superstition.

Still, there was no lack of skeptics. The following were the first to oppose the spiritistic madness: the noted chemist, Chevreul; the even more celebrated English physicist, Faraday; the previously cited founder of modern hypnotism, the English surgeon, Braid; his compatriot, Carpenter; and in Russia, Tarkhanov.[1] These men drew the attention of the scientific world to the so-called ideomotor acts and demonstrated that these acts explain all the movements of the spiritistic tables, as well as many other mysterious phenomena of the same order.

What then is an ideomotor act? We will demonstrate it in several examples. When we think, there are no visible movements whatsoever accompanying our thinking activity. But this does not mean that there are altogether no movements. It is possible, by utilizing special methods of observation, to detect certain movements. For instance, a subject is asked to hold in his hand a cord with some light weight attached to

---

[1] See his *Dukh i telo* (Spirit and Body), St. Petersburg, 1904, pp. 9-11, 63-65.

its end, forming thereby a kind of pendulum. The subject is then asked to concentrate his thought on some movement, the clockwise rotation of a pendulum, for instance. To the subject's amazement, the weight soon starts to move in a clockwise direction, describing a circle. What is going on here? It is this: the process of cortical excitation, which is connected with the thought of any movement, forces us to produce automatically the corresponding movement. This is what is called an ideomotor act. In the given case, the subject's hand unconsciously executes barely visible rotary movements, which force the suspended weight to take up the same movements. As is to be expected, the intensity of an ideomotor act varies with each individual, but the ability itself is inherent in all of us, without exception.[2] This phenomenon was already observed by the ancient Romans and used by them on occasion in augury. Here, for instance, is one example of such use in telling fortunes. The fortune-teller holds a thread, with a ring tied to it, over a cup, on the brim of which letters of the alphabet are arranged. Gradually the ring begins to swing, in the precise direction the fortune-teller expects. If this fortune-teller is secretly thinking of someone, the ring, as it touches the letters, will spell out the name of that person. Here the operative factor is not external suggestion but autosuggestion. The same thing happens when the cup is replaced by a saucer. Some fortune-tellers take a large sheet of paper

[2] Chevreul was the first (1812) to give the above explanation of the movement of the pendulum: "There exists a connection between some movements and thought, even though this thought is not the will which directs the muscular organs."

and write down the letters of the alphabet at random. A tea saucer is then placed upside down over the sheet of paper, and fortune-tellers put their fingers on the saucer, whereupon, to their amazement, they sometimes receive a more or less appropriate answer to a question mentally posed by them: the saucer, pushed slightly by the unconscious movements of the fortune-tellers themselves, successively stops near those letters of the alphabet which, when combined, give the words and whole sentences expected by them. In this case superstitious people are, so to speak, their own deluders, believing that they are receiving a reply from their guardian "spirit;" whereas, actually, they themselves are unconsciously answering their own questions.

With the aid of an ingeniously devised instrument for registering physical movement, Faraday, as long ago as 1853, demonstrated that the hands of the participants in spiritistic séances impart to the table a series of unconscious ideomotor jerks. Despite the insignificant force of each such jerk, in the aggregate they can be sufficient to set into movement even a fairly heavy table, just as a child, by a series of weak pulls on a rope, can set into motion a very heavy bell.

Following Faraday, the problem was studied by the psychophysiologist, Lehmann, who devised a method of recording the hand-movements of séance participants by means of a kymograph — a drum covered with smoked paper and set into rotary motion by a clock mechanism. The hand-movements of every séance participant were recorded on the smoked paper as curves. Analysis of such curves, obtained both prior to the onset of and during the table's movements, enabled Lehmann to explain how nonsimultaneous and variously directed ide-omotor jerks, communicated to a table by several séance partici-pants, may, in summation, cause it to move and slightly rock. Such slight rockings tap out letters of the alphabet being read aloud by one of the participants. As in fortune-telling with a saucer, connected sentences containing the answer to the ques-tion put to the "spirit" are sometimes obtained in this way. The role of the "spirit" is played, without his being aware of it, by the so-called medium, that is, by that séance participant whose ability for ideomotor action is more highly developed than that of the others. Let us, however, quote Lehmann, an expert on this question:

"I have frequently observed that, when the [séance] par-ticipants were uncertain, the first movements [of the table] were very hesitant, until something like the beginning of some word appeared. Then things accelerated, because the partici-pants' ideas became more definite; the terminal letters of the word appeared very quickly. At the beginning of each word hesitancy recurred, until there appeared a hint of a sentence that was clear to all, whereupon the end of the sentence came very quickly and without hesitation."[3] It is all quite different when a medium participates. He takes complete charge of the table, and in the tapped-out answers are revealed his own ideas, in part conscious, in part not. Out of this, says Dr. Lehmann, come the communications told about in accounts of spiritistic séances. However, even here the impression of some-thing miraculous depends on the séance participants' ignorance

---

[3] A. Lehmann, *Illustrirovannaya istoria sueveriy i volshebstva ot drev-nosti do nashikh dney* (Illustrated History of Superstition and Magic from Antiquity to the Present), p. 443.

of that psychophysiological phenomenon — ideomotor action which brings about these spiritistic "miracles."

Everything I have said refers, of course, only to cases where the participants in the séance tap out answers to their own questions "honestly," by means of unconscious ideomotor jerks. But this occurs rarely. Far more often, spiritistic séances are converted into an arena for the most shameless frauds, perpetrated by either some prankster or professional medium, who is paid a sizeable fee for a séance. In the mid-seventies of the last century, when addiction to spiritism was widespread, the eminent Russian chemist, D. I. Mendeleev, proposed that the Society of Physicists at St. Petersburg University establish a special commission for an examination of mediumistic phenomena. "The pursuit of table-turning, conversation with invisible beings, etc.," he wrote in his proposal, "threatens to spread mysticism, which can alienate many from a healthy outlook on things and reinforce superstition.... In order to counteract the spread of an unfounded doctrine and the present sterile dealing with mediumistic phenomena, these phenomena should not be ignored; they should, in my opinion, be accurately examined." The commission, composed of distinguished scientists and headed by Mendeleev himself, worked for nearly a year. Celebrated mediums were invited from abroad. Séances were conducted under conditions precluding the possibility of fraud. A manometric table, designed by Mendeleev, was constructed which accurately registered every manual pressure on it, even the weakest, by the participants in the séance.[4] But

---

[4] For a description and detailed account of the manometric table, see D. I. Mendeleev's book, *Materialy dlya suzhdenia spiritisma* (Materials for the Appraisal of Spiritism).

spirits flee from science as, according to a popular proverb, the devil flees from incense. The celebrated mediums forthwith faded away or, on attempting a demonstration, were exposed as frauds. The commission published its conclusion, which was devastating to spiritism. It ended with these words: "Spiritistic phenomena originate from unconscious movements or conscious deception, and spiritistic doctrine (belief in spirits) is superstition."

Friedrich Engels, too, passed devastating judgment against this superstition in his well-known article, "Natural Science in the World of Spirits," directed against very prominent naturalists of the period who had not escaped the spiritistic epidemic. Here he shows, by examples, how "the empirical contempt for dialectic is punished by the sacrifice of some of the soberest empiricists to the most primitive of all superstitions, contemporary spiritism." Engels ends his article with the following witty remark of the well-known English biologist Huxley: "The only good thing which, in my opinion, can be gained from a demonstration of the truth of 'spiritism' is a new argument against suicide. Better to live as a street sweeper than as a deceased one to chatter nonsense through the lips of some medium, who gets a guinea a séance."[5]

In his comedy, *The Fruits of Enlightenment,* the great literary genius, Leo Tolstoy, ridiculed the enthusiasm of the educated layers of society for spiritism. But the spiritistic fever continued. In 1912 there were some two thousand officially

---

[5] K. Marx and F. Engels, *Sochinenia* (Works), XX, pp. 382, 383. (The quotations given above are based on the translation from the German by Sidney Hook, "Natural Science and Spooks," *Marxist Quarterly,* Vol. I, No. 1, 1937 — Tr.)

registered spiritistic circles in Russia; the number abroad was even larger.[6] Truly, from blind faith to madness is only one step; no wonder even Tertullian, one of the first Christian theologians, once said: I believe it just because believing it is absurd![7]

Only the Soviet system, with its systematic mass inculcation of the achievements of dialectical materialism and the concrete sciences, has, once and for all, put an end to spiritism, as also to many other dangerous forms of superstition, by undermining their socio-political base.

Thus, the only thing worth attention in the phenomena of swinging pendulums, roaming saucers, and tapping tables is ideomotor behavior, explainable by the fact that concentrated thought on, or expectation of, some movement leads to the unconscious execution of this movement, even if in a very weak, at times barely perceptible, form. There is nothing mysterious in this. I. M. Sechenov maintained that thought is a reflex, more or less inhibited in its terminal, motor part, a reflex with a weakened terminus, and the arc of such a reflex passes through the neurons of the "psychic organ" — the cerebral cortex.[8] Ideomotor action is an excellent illustration of this idea of Sechenov.

---

[6] For more details, see the article by M. Shakhnovich, "Sotsialniye korni spiritisma" (The Social Roots of Spiritism), *Voinstvuyushchiy ateism*, No. 11 (1931), p. 21.

[7] The exact quotation is "It is certain because it is impossible," often incorrectly quoted as "I believe it because it is impossible." See "Tertullian," Columbia Encyclopedia, 3rd ed.—Tr.

[8] I. M. Sechenov, *Refleksy golovnovo mozga: izbranniye filosofskie i psikhologicheskie proizvedenia* (Brain Reflexes: Selected Philosophical and Psychological Works), Moscow, 1947.

It has now been shown, by precise experiments involving electrographic registration of impulses of excitation, that the thought of any movement or visual object, connected with a definite movement, is accompanied by the emergence of a rhythmic series of impulses in the muscles which would execute the movement thought of.[9] These impulses are transmitted to the muscles along the pyramidal nervous pathways, through those cortical neurons whose activity is connected with the motor thought entertained by the subject. For example, the mere thought of any high object, say the spire on top of the Leningrad Admiralty, is accompanied by the appearance of impulses of excitation in those ocular muscles whose contraction turns the eyes upward. A sufficiently sensitive galvanometer can also detect the weak electrical currents which accompany the impulses of excitation on thinking words (implicit speech). For this, electrodes connected with a galvanometer must be attached to the lips, tongue, and laryngeal muscles: the organs that realize the act of speech.

Recently, members of the Moscow Prosthetic and Orthopedic Institute made ingenious use of bioelectric currents in constructing a remarkable model of a functioning human hand. The hand is made of metal with mobile fingers. Its mechanism is connected by wires to a circular current-detector, worn as a bracelet on the arm of any subject. The mechanical hand executes the same movements which the subject thinks of at the given moment. For instance: the moment he thinks of making a fist, the artificial hand will do the same thing. This

---

[9] E. Jacobson, "Electrical Measurements of Neuromuscular States during Mental Activities," *American Journal of Physiology,* XCI (1930), p. 567

technical "miracle" comes about in the following way: at the thought of the movement to be made, the brain sends impulses of excitation to the appropriate muscles of the hand, that is, bioelectric currents which cause contraction of these muscles. The manual bioelectric currents which are picked up by the current-detector are transmitted to an amplifier which includes special equipment for putting into motion the fingers of the artificial hand. Thus, man's ideomotor activity can direct a machine — today by means of wires: tomorrow, conceivably without wires, through utilization of electromagnetic transmission[10] (see illustration on page 211).

The researches of Soviet physiologists (V. V. Yefimov and others) have demonstrated that entertaining movement thoughts not only produces biocurrents and weak contractions of the appropriate muscles, but is also accompanied by modification of their functional state: improved blood supply and nutrition, heightened excitability. More than that, entertaining motor thoughts puts into a state of functional readiness the whole integrated complex of the internal organs of cardiovascular, respiratory and secretory activity which ordinarily participate in the actual realization of functional behavior. In the given case, central nervous influences are transmitted along special sympathetic nerve fibers to the skeletal musculature, and also to the internal organs.

---

[10] See the article "Biotok upravlyaet machinoy" (Biocurrent Directs a Machine), *Izvestia*, Sept. 6, 1958; a more detailed account is given in the journal *Tekhnika — molodezhi*, No. 4, 1958, and a scientific exposition of the problem in an article by A. E. Kobrinsky, "Ispolzovanie biotokov dlya tseley upravlenia" (The Use of Biocurrents for Central Purposes), *Izvestia Akademii nauk SSSR, Otdel tekhnicheskikh nauk, Energetika i avtomatika*, No. 3 1959, p. 151.

Remarkably, involuntary movements may be produced not only by thoughts of which the subject is fully aware, but also by motor and visual images which the subject does not consciously experience at the given moment. There are, for instance, certain people who, during lively conversation, mechanically draw various figures, write words and snatches of sentences, unaware of what they have drawn or written. From this the highest degree of development of ideomotor behavior, known as graphic automatism, takes its origin. Spiritists value this rarely-met ability highly, fancying that the "writing medium" acts under the inspiration of an outside "spirit." Actually, automatic writing simply reveals the writer's repressed thoughts and desires, his forgotten and half-forgotten impressions.

Ideomotor behavior also explains another phenomenon, at first sight incomprehensible and long known under the incorrect and confusing designation of "mind-reading." Today this phenomenon is publicly demonstrated under the same designation and creates among naive viewers the impression of something new and unusual.[11] The demonstration of "mind reading" is conducted in the following manner: the participants (or one of them) think up some more or less complicated thing to do in the absence of the diviner (percipient) — for instance, to find a hidden object, to do something with it, or to transfer it to someone. This plan of action may be very complicated and confused. Now, one of the participants, who knows the planned task, makes contact with the "diviner" either by taking

---

[11] In prerevolutionary Russia, O. I. Feldman, a well-known hypnotist of the period, had great success with such demonstrations. Currently such demonstrations by Wolf Messing have attained wide popularity.

him by the wrist firmly or even by holding onto a tight lace, the other end of which is in the hands of the diviner. The guide (inductor) must concentrate all his attention on what has been proposed for the diviner to fulfill. The latter moves forward, now hesitatingly and often changing direction, now resolutely and quickly heading in the right direction. To the great amazement of the audience, he gradually fulfills the task set. What is involved here?

Public demonstrations of this kind were first conducted by Brown, an American, as long ago as 1874. His followers acquainted European audiences with these exhibitions. Their success was sensational and attracted the attention of scientists. Beard in America, Carpenter in England, and Preier in Germany independently discovered the secret of these spectacular exhibitions. In Russia, in the early nineties, the Society of Experimental Psychology appointed a special commission for the examination of these phenomena.[12] Opinion was unanimous: this is not "mind-reading" but "muscle-reading." In other words, the diviner is led in his actions by ideomotor signals sent to him involuntarily by the guide, who is concentrating on the movements and the direction the diviner should take for fulfillment of the task set. For instance: the diviner must find a hidden object. If he moves in the wrong direction, he senses a barely perceptible resistance on the part of the guide. If he is moving in the right direction, the guide, too, moves freely, directing the future action of the diviner with externally imperceptible jerks which the guide, himself, is not aware of.

---

[12] The commission's protocols were published in the journal *Voprosy filosofii i psikhologii*, 1892.

The success of these exhibitions is predicated on two conditions: first, the guide should have sufficiently expressed ideomotor behavior; secondly, the diviner must be sufficiently receptive to hardly perceptible motor signals to have a chance of having his actions guided by them. Preier, in connection with this, relates that on several occasions he served as guide for some of the most famed "mind-readers" and not once had any one of them divined the tasks he had set for them; this was because, knowing what it was all about, Preier tried, as much as possible, to hold back his ideomotor behavior.

Various established methods — for instance, utilization of the pendulum already mentioned in this chapter — can be used to reveal beforehand whether there exists sufficient ideomotor ability for the successful conduct of these exhibitions. In our experiments we used a so-called pneumatic platform, consisting of two wooden triangles, set one on top of the other; wooden blocks were placed between the two base angles of the triangles: under the third angle, to the rear of the subject standing on the platform, there was placed an elastic rubber balloon, connected by a pneumatic mechanism with a Marey tambour known to all physiologists; a lever from the tambour registered on the revolving drum of a kymograph a jagged curve which reflected the involuntary swayings of the subject.[13] A rise in the curve corresponded to swaying forward, a decline to swaying

---

[13] For a detailed description of the pneumatic platform, see the article by A. I. Bronshtein, "K metodike registrazii dvigatelnoy reakzii u cheloveka" (On a Method of Registering Human Motor Reaction), in the collection *Voprosy izuchenia i vospitania lichnosti* (Problems in the Study and Training of the Individual), *Trudy Instituta mozga*, Nos. 1-2 (Leningrad, 1930), p. 98.

backward. A subject was given instructions: "Imagine that you are falling backward, that you are being pulled back." The curve of many subjects — instantly or gradually — began to decline, testifying to strong expressiveness in them of ideomotor behavior. Such individuals make good guides in "muscle-reading" exhibitions. The curve of other subjects either showed practically no change following receipt of instructions, or intensified swaying in both directions; in some cases there was observed even a distorted reaction: the swaying movements decreased. This means that the subjects were revealing a negative attitude to the instructions given them: the subjects were unconsciously inhibiting even those weak swaying movements which were registered prior to the receipt of instructions. Of course, such individuals are not satisfactory for exhibitions of "muscle reading."[14]

That there is no "mind reading" whatever in any of the described exhibitions is attested also by the fact that, when all possible accomplices are excluded from an exhibition, the best "diviner," lacking a guide, can accomplish nothing. At public demonstrations, exhibitions without contact are sometimes successful, but there is no guarantee whatever that their conduct was foolproof and without outside assistance.[15] Furthermore.

---

[14] See L. L. Vasiliev and G. Yu. Belitsky. "O tipakh protekania ideomotornoy reaktsii" (Patterns of Ideomotor Reaction), *Byulleten eksperimentalnoy biologii i meditsiny,* XVII, 1-2 (1940), p. 26.

[15] V. G. Messing gives another explanation: "I frequently perform tasks set in the minds of others without direct contact with an inductor, and even when blindfolded. In such cases I may be guided by the rate of the inductor's breathing, the beat of his pulse, the timbre of his voice, the character of his gait, etc." See V. G. Messing, "Chtenie muskulov, a ne mysley" (Muscle Reading, Not Mind Reading), *Tekhnika — molodezhi,* No. 1 (1960), p. 32.

although they may execute the most complicated motor tasks, "diviners" refuse the simplest tasks of visual character. "Mind readers" on the stage, for instance, are not capable of divining such conjured visual images as "red rose," "white horse," or the like, since in such cases not even the most refined perceptivity of ideomotor signals is of any help.

"Mind-reading" exhibitions and their scientific explanation facilitated the revival of interest in so-called telepathy — an ancient notion that under certain conditions the psychic experiences of one person can be transmitted to another at a distance, and that such transmission takes place, as it were, directly from one brain to another without the participation of external sense organs.

Idealists cite the phenomenon of so-called transmission of thought as demonstration of the independence of a psychic principle, of the possibility of the existence of the psyche outside the brain, independently of matter. In their view, thought may separate from the brain and, not beholden to the categories of time, space, causality, or any other laws of nature, be transmitted to another brain. This is the alleged consistence of "unmediated transmission of thought," in other words, "mental suggestion." Quite obviously, such a notion does not differ essentially from primitive animism, and is in basic contradiction to all the achievements of a truly scientific physiology and psychology. These sciences prove indisputably that thought, like the entire psyche, is simply a property of highly organized matter, appearing at a definite stage in the latter's development, and is, therefore, as inseparable from its substratum — the brain — as, say, the whiteness of the paper in front of me is inseparable from the paper itself.

The problem of mental suggestion, when interpreted idealistically, loses all scientific sense and is turned into superstition. But, it is necessary to say that there is yet another approach to the given problem — one which does not hide in itself anything of the unscientific, the mystical, and which can be verified by rigorously conducted experiments. Outstanding scientists, certainly in no way idealists (for example, V. M. Bekhterev and P. P. Lazarev), assumed the possibility of mental suggestion; understanding it as "brain broadcasting," as the result of the transmission of electromagnetic energy from one functioning brain to another. At public lectures on such topics as "Sleep and Dreams," "Hypnosis and Suggestion," "The Brain and the Psyche," the greater part of the slips of paper sent up to the lecturer by the audience ask this question: Is telepathy possible? Does "brain broadcasting" exist? At the same time the questioners often adduce "remarkable occurrences" from their own lives or from the lives of relatives and friends, setting them forth sometimes with an obvious coating of religious or occult ideas.

We deem it, therefore, necessary to devote the next chapter to an examination of the contemporary judgment of the scientific problem of mental suggestion and of the superstitious ideas connected with it.

CHAPTER VI

Does
"Brain Broadcasting"
Exist?

CHAPTER VI

Does
"Brain Broadcasting"
Exist?

BELIEF IN THE EXISTENCE of this phenomenon is extremely widespread. In literary works, in the biographies of eminent men, in historical memoirs, in magazine articles and press reports of practically all peoples from all times there are scattered descriptions of diverse events from daily life designated as "telepathy," "unmediated thought transmission," "mental suggestion," "brain broadcasting," and so forth. In general form, these events may be expressed this way: if at a given moment A dies or is in mortal danger or is experiencing some important agitating event, then frequently another person (call him B), who is bound to A by ties of kinship, love or friendship and who is far away from A, experiences at that very time a psychic state which more or less reflects the event which the person A is experiencing.

The descriptions of such events are very often put into mystical form and are interpreted as mysterious "messages" or "forewarnings" that the "soul" of a near one is about to pass into a "better world." Understandably, therefore, telepathy was for a long time considered to be an article of faith, rather than a subject for study and scientific investigation. Not until the middle of the nineteenth century did a few scientists venture to show interest in the subject. The year 1876 can be considered as the turning point, when at a session of the British Association of Scientists, the well-known English physicist, Barrett, a student of Faraday and Tyndall, delivered an address on "unmediated thought transmission." Following this, systematic research was begun of cases of so-called spontaneous telepathy reported in daily life. In its behalf, the Society for Psychical Research was formed in London in 1882 — an organization still in existence. Every case of spontaneous telepathy was carefully studied by members of this Society; obligatory recording of all written documents and the interrogation of witnesses were demanded and cases so corroborated were pursued to the limits of inquiry. Similar societies were afterwards founded in many other European countries, in the United States and Asia. In 1920 the International Committee for Psychical Research was formed. It organized several congresses, at which were discussed numerous papers devoted to the study of the mysterious phenomena of the human psyche — primarily telepathy.

In capitalist countries the undiminished, in fact, progressively growing, interest in telepathic phenomena is nourished by the prevailing religious belief. But even in our own country interest is strong and to a certain extent is supported by literary works, not only classical, but also contemporary Soviet, in which are recited with great vividness incidents clearly telepathic in nature. The sketch "Two Mothers,"[1] published in the periodical *Ogonyok* (No. 7, 1941), is an example. O. O. Ostrovskaya gives an ingenuous account of her "premonition" concerning the death of her son, the noted Soviet writer, Nikolay Ostrovsky. This story is very typical of the incidents called spontaneous telepathy. We therefore reproduce it in its entirety.

"I am a simple peasant woman, don't be offended if I tell you my dream. I am asleep at home, in Sochi, and have a dream: planes are flying over the sea, many planes, and they are making so much noise my ears hurt. I realize that war has started. I run outside and look: there stands my Kolya, quite healthy, in a military greatcoat and helmet, and holding a rifle. Around him are trenches, holes, and barbed wire. I want to ask Kolya about the war, then realize that he's standing guard, and mustn't be asked questions. I want to go back to the house, but the holes keep widening, the barbed wire entangles my feet, holds me back, I want to scream — and can't.

"Then I awoke, and I pondered: that was a bad dream, something surely must have happened to Kolya in Moscow. I thought: I shall go for tickets and travel to Moscow to Kolya. I was getting ready to go for the ticket when suddenly I got a letter from Kolya. He wrote that he's better, that soon he'll be back, and that in the spring he'll stay with me. I read, but anxiety did not leave me. I tried to persuade myself: well, where will you go, old woman? Why go, if Kolya writes that everything is fine? And so I did not go for the ticket.

---

[1] "Dve materi."

"I went to bed that night (around eleven o'clock), I heard something, someone knocking. 'Are you in bed, Olga Osipovna?'

" 'Yes,' I answered, 'I am in bed,' and I recognized the voice of an acquaintance from the Gorkom.[2]

" 'Get up,' he said. 'Kolya is worse, and we want to send you to Moscow.'

"Right there my heart sank to my knees. I lay there, and said only that the night train had already gone and there would not be another until morning.

" 'Never mind, we'll send you by trolley,' the man said.

"But I knew how the trolley jolts and I flatly refused to go. Then he came a little closer to the door and said:

" 'Kolya has died, Kolya is no more!' and burst into tears..."

Hundreds of similar instances have been recorded.[3] For comparison, I reproduce another instance, drawn from the documents of the aforementioned London Society. "On the day of his death my father, as usual, left the house at three-thirty to walk in the garden and the fields. Seven or eight minutes had not gone by when, in conversation with my wife and sister, I suddenly felt a strong urge to go to my father. [We had been talking about a planned after-dinner call on our neighbor, and we had not mentioned father at all.] The conviction that I must go to him became overwhelming. I insisted that everyone in the house go out to look for him. The others

---

[2] Abbreviation for *Gorodskoy komitet*, City Committee — Tr.

[3] For example, C. Flammarion, the noted French astronomer, collected over a thousand through use of a questionnaire.

objected, saying that my alarm was unreasonable. However, a search was begun, and my father was actually found dead."[4]

How should one regard stories of this kind? Let me first of all emphatically underscore the fact that they are by no means necessarily connected with death, or some intense psychic experience involving near ones. There are records of allegedly telepathic transmissions of the most commonplace, not in the least tragic, trivialities of daily life. Here is an example, taken from the collection of the same London Society (case No. 59): "One recent morning, as I was engaged in some light chores, I saw mentally a small basket of willow twigs with five eggs in it; two of them were very clean, larger than usual, oblong and yellowish; one was completely round and white, but dirty; the remaining two had no distinctive marks. I wondered what meaning this sudden unimportant vision could have? I never think of such trifles. However, this basket lodged in my mind, and occupied it for several minutes.

"Some two hours later I went to have breakfast in another room. I was immediately struck by the remarkable similarity of the eggs in the egg-cups on the table to the two oblong eggs I had just seen in my imagination. 'Why are you staring at these eggs so intently?' asked my wife, and was greatly amazed to learn that I knew the number of eggs her mother had sent her half an hour ago. She then brought the other three eggs, and I saw both the soiled egg and the recognizable basket. Later I learned that the eggs had been gathered by my mother-

---

[4] E. Gurney, F. Myers and F. Podmore, *Phantasms of the Living*, Case No. 79, London, 1886. (Russian translation, *Prizhiznennye prizraki* [Phantoms in One's Lifetime], St. Petersburg, 1895.)

in-law, who put them in the basket and sent them to me. Later, she herself related that, of course, at that time she was thinking about me. She did this at ten o'clock in the morning, at the precise moment of the vision's appearance."

In his articles, "On the Transmission of Thought over Distance," Mark Twain, the famous American humorist, describes many such "apparently meaningless" events out of his own life, treating them by no means humorously but in all seriousness.[5] He is especially intrigued by the frequently occurring instances in his life of "premonitions of meeting a familiar person." Suddenly, out of the blue, some acquaintance, man or woman, comes to mind; a minute or two later you meet just this person on the street. Such coincidences sometimes assume the form of an illusion, "sham recognition": you mistake a stranger coming toward you from a distance for a good acquaintance — N; it then appears that the man you are meeting is not N, and doesn't look like N at all; but you walk a few dozen paces further and there in front of you appears the true N.

In his novel, *Smoke*, I. S. Turgenev described with psychological acuteness a similar situation. After breaking off with the young lady, "Litvinov had but one thought: to see Irina. He set out to look for her." But he did not find her and "he plodded away" "empty as a tambourine": fragmentary thoughts and recollections followed each other in disorder. "Suddenly something wafted over him, something intangible but definite; if a breath of air had come from a falling shadow it could not

---

[5] Mark Twain, *Polnoe sobranie sochineniy* (Complete Works), Vols. II-III, St. Petersburg, 1911.

have been more elusive. Instantly he sensed that this was Irina drawing near. And truly she did appear, just a few steps away, arm in arm with another woman; their eyes met."[6]

Perhaps some of my readers have had similar experiences. But can these everyday occurrences serve as scientific proof of the real existence of telepathy, of "brain broadcasting?" Of course not. They cannot serve as true cases because one cannot entirely rule out the possibility of chance coincidence — of two persons involved in the same experience at approximately the same time. Improbable coincidences occur sometimes in everyday life — coincidences in which telepathy, even if it existed, could play no role whatever. I have myself recorded in a special notebook thirty-four such hardly probable coincidences, all more or less of the same kind, during the past twenty-two years. At the very least the following entry can serve as an example: "On January 17, 1940 I was looking through *Leningradskaya Pravda* of that date and simultaneously listening with half an ear to what the radio announcer was saying. On the first page of the newspaper I started to read an article, entitled 'A High Reward'. It listed the surnames of the soldiers and officers (six in all) who had distinguished themselves in battles with the White Finns. From among them the name Mazepa, which is today very rare, caught my eye, and literally at the same moment the announcer spoke the same name, Mazepa. He was announcing the theatrical repertory for the next few days and, among other performances, named Tchaikovsky's opera *Mazepa.*

---

[6] I. S. Turgenev, Dym (Smoke), Moscow: GIKHL, 1955, p. 131.

Audiences at lectures on mysterious phenomena of the psyche frequently cite travelers' accounts of the tricks performed by Indian fakirs as indicative of the power of mental suggestion. Reports of such tricks have repeatedly appeared in the press. One, for instance, is the following eyewitness account by A. N. Skalovsky, a Czarist Vice-Admiral, from his book, *Microcosm and Macrocosm:*

"Sitting on the deck [of a Russian man-of-war], and surrounded by spectators, the fakir takes a pot, apparently filled with earth. After covering the pot with a cloth, in plain view of everybody, he manipulates something over the pot [under the cloth] for ten to fifteen minutes, as if strenuously kneading. Intense concentration and tension are written on his face. He then removes his hands from under the cloth, and the astonished onlookers see the cloth rising higher and higher; in a little while the fakir pulls off the cloth, and his amazed audience sees that some kind of bush has sprouted in the pot. The fakir then asks for a pitcher of water and pours sand into the bottom of this pitcher. Then, again in plain view, he takes up a handful of the wet sand and squeezes it hard; his face is contorted; it is obvious that he is making a great effort. He opens his hand — it is completely dry, and the handful of sand is as dry as dust. The author personally witnessed these tricks."[7] Skalovsky adds that no one had succeeded in recording any such phenomena on photographic plates.

Understandably, the tricks of fakirs cannot be accepted, any more than those of others, as sufficient proof of the existence of "brain broadcasting." A scientific resolution of the

---

[7] A. N. Skalovsky *Mikrokosmos i makrokosmos* (Microcosm and Macrocosm), St. Petersburg, 1913, p. 86.

problem may be gained only through experimentation on mental suggestion conducted in accordance with all the rules of modern science. Psychiatrists, physiologists, and physicists began to conduct such experimentation toward the end of the last century. At first, the methods of experimental telepathy were very simple and were applied to a large number of subjects; the findings were evaluated in terms of the probability theory. For example, the noted French physiologist, Charles Richet,[8] conducted numerous experiments in the guessing of playing cards concentrated on [by others]. According to his data, the number of correct guesses so tried always exceeds the number of guesses as calculated through the probability theory, but the difference is not statistically significant. For example: the probability theory indicates that out of 2,997 trials there should occur by chance 732 correct responses; "telepathically," there were 789. A more significant result was obtained in some cases, but the persons tested were uncommon ones. Such experiments led to the conclusion that (as is true also of verbal suggestion) not all persons by far lend themselves to mental suggestion, and that to extend the experiments it would be necessary to pick the most suitable, the most suggestible subjects.

Richet's experiments with the application of the probability theory were further developed in England (by Dr. Soal), and in the United States (by Dr. Rhine), with, however, this difference: instead of playing cards, they used cards with five sharply distinguishable black figures against a white background. On each card was drawn one of the following five

---

[8] Charles Richet, "La Suggestion mentale et le calcule des probabilites," *Revue philosophique*, XVIII, 1884, p. 609.

figures: a square, a circle, wavy lines, a star, and a cross. In experiments, a pack of twenty-five such cards was used, each figure being repeated five times. These cards were proposed by Dr. Rhine's collaborator, Dr. Zener, and at the present time have gained international distribution. Telepathic experiments utilizing Zener's cards are being conducted in various countries. The results of these uniform experiments can be easily collated and compared with each other.

The sender (the inductor) and the receiver of mental suggestion (the percipient) sit across from each other at a table, in the middle of which stands a cardboard or plywood screen measuring 18 x 24 inches. The screen prevents the percipient from seeing the inductor and the pack of cards in his hands. The inductor carefully shuffles the cards (not less than four or five times) and explains to the percipient how he is to guess the cards and inscribe his responses on the recording sheet lying before him.

When the percipient signals (by speaking or knocking) that he is ready for the test, the inductor forthwith takes the top card from the pack and looks at it. The percipient writes his response on the paper and signals again. The inductor places the first card on the table face down and takes a second card from the pack, looking at it until he hears the next signal of the percipient, and so on, until the whole pack is used up. Then the inductor records the order of the cards on a sheet of paper, collates his recording sheet with the percipient's and inscribes the number of guesses. Such tallying is conducted with the participation of the percipient, in order to sustain his interest in these rather monotonous experiments.

Each experiment (or rather, each series) consists of twenty-five trials. At each sitting the percipient has to go through a minimum of four such series, with long enough intervals to avoid fatigue. But a more reliable number of series will have to go up to 10 or more. A great deal, too, depends on the conditions under which the experiment is conducted. Such experiments should be carried out at that speed which is preferred by the percipient himself. He must not be tied to too rapid or too slow a tempo. The subject must be interested, and confident of success; if he is not, it is necessary to encourage him to achieve success — to try for results better than chance would give. The probability of success by pure guessing is 20%, or five correct responses per twenty-five cards. That is, in four series (100 trials) 20 correct responses would occur by chance alone. The success of the percipient is measured by the number of correct responses exceeding that number.

The following table, compiled on the basis of probability theory, enables the experimenter to evaluate the results obtained by him.

NUMBER OF SERIES OF 25 TRIALS EACH	NUMBER OF CORRECT RESPONSES		SCORES STRIKINGLY EXCEEDING CHANCE
	CHANCE SCORE	TYPICAL SCORES EXCEEDING CHANCE	
4	20	26	32
10	50	63	69
50	250	279	293
100	500	540	560

By observing all the conditions we have noted above, and over a large series of experiments, English and American parapsychologists have repeatedly obtained a large number of correct responses whose probability of occurrence by chance alone is extremely low. For instance, in experiments with two young cousins (one of whom was inductor, the other percipient), Soal, after 15,000 trials, got for each pack of 25 cards an average of nearly nine correct responses instead of the five suggested by the probability theory. Twice in these experiments all twenty-five cards were guessed correctly in consecutive order; twenty-four cards were guessed correctly four times: and from twenty-three to nineteen cards, forty times. This result exceeds by many times what could have been expected from chance. For example, the probability of correctly naming by chance alone a sequence of 25 cards is quite negligible. This result may be obtained once out of 5^{25} trials ($5^{25} = 298,023,223,876,953,125$ — a truly astronomical figure!).

With individual subjects who are very receptive to mental suggestion, it is possible to evoke by such means things of even greater visual complexity — drawings, objects, words, and the like (not the five figures known in advance, as in the experiments with Zener's cards, but figures without limitation).

The subject is asked to draw on paper or to describe verbally all those visual images which might come to subject's mind during the experiment. Here is a successful experiment of this kind, taken from Dr. Tischner's book.[9] The subject, a woman, was placed behind a screen, covered, in addition, by a large shawl. The mental transmitter sat with his back to the screen at a distance of several meters from her. There were no mirrors in the room, and no other reflecting surfaces. Dr. Tischner himself conducted the experiment. He

[9] R. Tischner, *Über Telepathie und Hellsehen*, Munich, 1920.

would hand some object or other to the mental transmitter, and then record the verbal response of the subject. Here is the record of this experiment:

"Object of mental suggestion — scissors. The experiment begins at 8:14 AM. Two minutes later the subject begins to speak: 'This seems quite large to me. I am still too occupied with my own thoughts...now it seems to me to be a rather small, narrow, short object...as if somewhat twisted like a corkscrew...a knife maybe or something similar. It seems to me to be very difficult to recognize...Unfortunately, I am not very attentive...the day's impressions are always interfering. Now I see the image of Mme. Tischner. Is it a coin? [Dr. Tischner answered that it wasn't]. Now I see it as something round, sparkling,...does it always sparkle?...Now it is like a ring...It is again as if of metal...It glitters, like glass or metal...round, yet extended in length...as if it were a pair of scissors...underneath are two little round pieces, and further it is extended...it must be a pair of scissors.' Then immediately (at 8:26 A.M.), the subject with an expression of confidence repeated: 'It is a pair of scissors!'"

In these experiments it is characteristic that the suggested image is induced in the mind of the person, who is tuning in only gradually on the projected suggestion, with mistakes and inaccuracies along the way until eventually he attains greater or lesser clarity. Often there results only an approximate, symbolic description or representation of the thing thought about (see Dr. Bruck's experiments).[10]

Certain mechanical devices are sometimes employed to

---

[10] C. Bruck, *Experimentelle telephathie,* Stuttgart, 1925.

facilitate these experiments. For instance: the percipient is given a so-called planchette, which is a small, easily movable board, set up on three legs, a fine pencil serving as one of the legs. The planchette is placed on a large sheet of paper; a subject, gifted with a special faculty for automatic movements, puts his hand on the planchette and, as if automatically and unconsciously, records with its help what the experimenter has mentally suggested to him.

Out of the great number of similar investigations, the experiments of the American writer, Upton Sinclair, in mental transmission of drawings to his wife, Mary Sinclair, gained wide fame. Upton Sinclair gave an account of these experiments in his book, *Mental Radio*[11], which attracted the attention of the distinguished American physiologist, MacDougall, the parapsychologist, Walter Prince, and other scientists. Prince wrote a book in which he presents data as evidence of the trustworthiness of Sinclair's experiments — the testimony of eye-witnesses and of the participants of these experiments.[12] The inductor was not Sinclair alone; in several sessions a relative of the percipient served as inductor. Mental suggestion originated in another room, and for several experiments in another house thirty miles away. These experiments were especially successful when, to use her own expression, Mary was "on the brink of sleep" and the drawings that were transmitted appeared in her drowsy consciousness in the form of visual images.

---

[11] Pasadena Station, 1930.
[12] *The Sinclair Experiments Demonstrating Telepathy*, Boston, 1932.

It should be stated that this and similar experiments do not lend themselves to strict statistical treatment and are therefore not as convincing for the establishment of the existence of mental transmission as quantitative experiments with Zener's cards. But, in compensation, the experiments with mental transmission of drawings, reinforced by the results of experiments with cards, serve better to clarify the psychological features of telepathic perception (receptivity). In this connection, the percipient's errors in the representation or realization of drawings perceived by the inductor are especially instructive. Here are two examples from Sinclair's book:

> The inductor draws a smoking volcano; the percipient draws the same thing, but labels her drawing quite differently: "a large black cockroach with horns." Word and content do not match! There are many analogous examples in the book. What do they tell us? Undoubtedly, that it is merely the visual image that is perceived telepathically, and not the concept, not the word, not thought in the exact meaning of the term.
>
> Such cases may be called telepathic reproduction of the inductor's drawing without its recognition. On the other hand, there occur instances where exactly the opposite is true — telepathic recognition of the inductor's drawing without its reproduction. Here is an example from the same source: The drawing of a monkey swinging from branch to branch was mentally projected. The percipient did not reproduce this rather complicated drawing, but, on the other hand, she recognized the category of images to which the drawing belonged. She wrote: "Buffalo or lion, tiger — wild animal."

Experiments in mentally hypnotizing and arousing the percipient testify to the same point. The most distinguished Soviet hypnologist, Prof. K. I. Platonov, who carried out many such experiments, writes: "It is important to note that when I exerted influence on the subject in the form of a mental command, 'Go to sleep!' — 'Sleep!' — the results were negative. But with visual representation on my part of the image and figure of the subject in hypnotized state (or, in the case of an awakening subject, with mental suggestion of awakening), the effect was always positive."[13]

This implies that the often used expressions, "mental transmission" and "mental suggestion", are not precise. Telepathically it is possible to transmit *only* visual, more rarely auditory, images, feelings, drives to action — that which Pavlov related to the first signal system — and *not* thoughts, connected with words, related to the second signal system.

This makes understandable why telepathic experiments are sometimes successful even in those cases when the inductor is, for example, French, and the percipient, Greek; with the Frenchman not knowing a word of Greek, and the Greek not knowing a word of French. Such experiments in the telepathic transmission of drawings were conducted on an international scale and produced results deserving attention.[14]

The main condition in the method of all these experiments is the exclusion, as far as can be managed, of the possi-

---

[13] From K. I. Platonov's letter to the author of this book. Quoted with Professor Platonov's permission.

[14] K. Konstantinides, "Telepatische Experimente zwischen Athen, Paris, Warschau und Wien," *Transactions of the Fourth International Congress for Psychical Research*, S. P. R., London, 1930, p. 215.

bility of perceiving the mentally transmitted task in the usual way — by way of the sense organs. Thus, for example, Dr. Brugmans at the Laboratory of Psychology in the University of Groningen (Holland) conducted the following experiments, quite complex in their design. Two rooms, one located above the other, were especially adapted for the experiments. In the floor of the darkened upper room a little opening was made into which two thick panes of glass were inserted, thereby blocking the passage of even loud sounds from the upper to the lower room. Through this opening, the experimenters, in the upper room, could observe what was happening in the brightly illuminated lower room where the subject had been placed. The experimenters could not see the subject himself, since during the experiment he was in a special closet-like booth, closed over on top, in front, and on the two sides. In front of this booth, directly under the glassed-over opening, stood a table on which was a cardboard representing a chess-board with forty-eight large squares, each bearing its appropriate chess designation. On this cardboard rested the hand of the subject thrust through a horizontal slit cut in the front wall of the booth. In this way, the subject could not see the cardboard, while the experimenters, though unable to see him, were able to follow his hand.

In each separate trial in the experiment, the experimenters, while looking down on the cardboard and the subject's hand, mentally suggested that he move his hand from one square of the chessboard to another — for instance, from square a2 to square c5. The choice of the square to which the subject was to move his hand was each time decided by lot.

During the course of these experiments one of the subjects — a student — especially attracted attention. In 60 out of 187 times he indicated with complete exactness the mentally projected square, which made 31 percent of the trials successful. In similar experiments, the same subject, stimulated by a pharmaceutical preparation which raised the excitability of the cerebral cortex, increased his score to 75 percent.

These experiments, published in 1922, attained widespread publicity. Analogous studies were undertaken in many countries, and a department for the special study of similar psychic phenomena was established at one of Holland's universities (in Utrecht). At the present time, special laboratories have been established for the same purpose in the United States, England, and several other countries: dissertations are being defended and conferences (symposiums) are called for the discussion of like problems of the human brain and psyche.[15]

Emerging scientific interest in the problem of mental suggestion was given great impetus by H. Hertz's discovery (in 1888) of electromagnetic waves and the subsequent progress of wireless telegraphy (A. S. Popov) and modern radio broadcasting, from which was derived the very term "brain broadcasting." The Academician P. P. Lazarev wrote about the possible role of electromagnetic waves in mental activity as follows:

---

[15] An index to the literature on parapsychological problems, including telepathy, compiled by G. Zorab (*Bibliography of Parapsychology*, New York, 1957) contains nearly one thousand titles. See also *Proceedings of Four Conferences of Parapsychological Studies*, Parapsychology Foundation, New York, 1957.

"The periodic [chemical] reactions taking place in the centers [of the brain] must be generating electromotive forces in the *area* of the centers. According to the electromagnetic theory of light, in transmitting the electric phenomena to the surface of the head, these electromagnetic forces must be accompanied by an electromagnetic wave, spreading with the speed of light in the surrounding medium. Every sensation, every act of movement must form waves, and the human head should radiate waves of great length (up to 30,000 kilometers) into the surrounding medium. What physiological role these waves may play, it is difficult to say; but it is possible that they may help us to explain the phenomena of suggestion [this can obviously only refer to nonverbal mental suggestion] as well as other, more complex phenomena in the psychic field."

These considerations, expressed by Academician P. P. Lazarev in 1922,[16] quickly found a certain basis in fact. Oscillating electrical potentials, which could be amplified and registered on an oscillograph in the form of the so-called electroencephalogram, were actually found on the surface of the human head.[17] Electroencephalography has now entered medical practice as a method helping to establish the correct diagnosis in several brain diseases. The research conducted over a number of years (1923 to 1929) by the Italian neurologist, Cazzamalli, in collaboration with physicists claims the

---

[16]See his *Fiziko-khimicheskie osnovy vysshey nervnoy deyatelnosti,* (The Physicochemical Foundations of Higher Nervous Activity) Moscow, 1922, p. 46.

[17] The first electroencephalogram was procured from warm-blooded animals through application of a string galvanometer by the Russian electrophysiologist, Professor Pravdich-Neminsky, as far back as 1913.

discovery of centimeter-long electromagnetic waves in the space around a subject's head.

For his experiments, Cazzamalli constructed an isolated room built on the principles of Faraday's cage. This room consisted of a wooden frame in the shape of a parallelepiped, the six sides of which were covered by lead sheets 1.5 mm. in thickness. Control experiments showed that the lead walls reliably shield the interior of the room from penetration by radio waves from the outside, which abound so richly in our earth's atmosphere today. The subject was introduced into the room through an opening in the ceiling, which was covered by a special shutter. Persons possessing high suggestibility and capable of falling into deep hypnosis served as subjects. In the room were a cot, a table, a chair, and also a sensitive radio receiver, tuned to the reception of metric, decimetric, or centimetric wave lengths. Reception was managed through a frame-antenna, set up inside the room and directed toward the subject. The radio receiver was connected by wire to earphones placed on the head of the experimenter, who was usually also inside the room, but during some experiments outside the room.

As long as the subject remained in the waking state, the radio receiver picked up no signals whatsoever. But as soon as the subject fell into hypnotic sleep and through verbal suggestion was brought to a state of emotional excitement (caused, for example, by hallucination through suggestion), sounds were heard in the earphones, indicating the emergence of radio-waves within the room. The character of the sounds was highly varied. Sometimes there was a roar, crackle, whistling; at other times there were musical tones resembling a violoncello, a flute, or human voice. Even normal mental activity — normal, that is, under stress — had a certain effect on the radio receiver. Later, Cazzamalli replaced the earphones with a string-galvanometer, which made it graphically possible to register on photographic tape the signals produced by the radio waves of the brain.

On the basis of these experiments, Cazzamalli arrived at the following conclusions: The human brain, during heightened activity, becomes the source of metric and, especially, decimetric and centrimetric electromagnetic waves. These brain radio-waves sometimes display aperiodicity; that is, variability of wave length, or have a similarity to retarded waves. Sometimes for a short time they appear as unretarded waves of definite frequency. According to Cazzamalli, brain radio-waves may be the physical agent which transmits mental suggestion from the brain of the experimenter to that of the subject.[18]

Cazzamalli's experiments and theoretical conclusions, and their possible significance for physiology and psychology, aroused great interest, but also a good deal of critical comment in both the foreign scientific press and our own. A critical analysis, from the point of view of physics, for example, may be found in an article by Professor A. Petrovsky.[19] An attempt, in which this author participated, was made to replicate Cazzamalli's experiments at the V. M. Bekhterev Institute of

---

[18] F. Cazzamalli, "Les Ondes électro-magnétiques en corrélation avec certaines phénomènes psycho-sensoriels," *Comptes rendues de III⁰ Congrès International de Recherches Psychiques,* Paris, 1928.
[19] "Telepsikhicheskie yavlenia i mozgoviye radiatsii" (Telepsychic Phenomena and Mental Radiation), *Telegrafia i telefonia bez provodov.* No. 34 (1926) p. 61.

the Brain in Leningrad. It produced no positive findings. We do not know whether any foreign investigators succeeded in obtaining positive findings and can only point to the successful disclosure, by two German physicists,[20] of an electromagnetic field of low frequency near contracting muscles in man and animals. This field was detected by means of a reception disk, connected through a three-valve amplifier with a string-galva- nometer. The frequency of the oscillations recorded on photo- graphic tape corresponded to the rhythm of the biocurrents entering into the contracting muscles from the central nervous system (about 50 cycles per second). Corresponding to this frequency are electromagnetic waves of very great length — nearly 6,000 kilometers — which P. P. Lazarev also considers as that physical agent which can effect mental suggestion.

Thus, two points of view were expressed on the form of electromagnetic energy that is produced by the functioning brain, issues into the surrounding medium, and having pene- trated into another brain, elicits there certain neuropsychic processes. According to Lazarev it was low-frequency electro- magnetic waves of very great length; according to Cazzamalli it was ultra-high-frequency waves of very short length. But even if we acknowledge the existence of both brain waves, one question still remains unclear. Are these brain waves capable of stimulating the cortex of another brain, and do they thereby activate in it neurophychic processes, directly and without participation of the sense organs?

We have the following data on the subject: The work

---

[20] See the article by F. Sauerbruch and W. Schumann in the journal *Zeitschrift für technische Physik* (Leipzig) No. 3 (1928), S.96, p.315.

of the noted physiologist V. Ya. Danilevsky demonstrated that under the influence of electromagnetic fields of low frequency (50-100 cycles per second) one can stimulate isolated nerve' and muscle tissue across distance and also heighten the excitability of the central nervous system in animals and man.[21] In our laboratory we recently succeeded in establishing in healthy subjects a conditioned reflex to the unsensed action of an electromagnetic field of low frequency (200 cycles per second).[22] This means that this physical factor is capable of acting upon the "organ of the psyche" — the cerebral cortex. There are analogous findings for ultra-high-frequency electromagnetic fields, though the mechanism of their action on living tissues is basically different from that of low-frequency fields. Thus, a member of P. P. Lazarev's school, established in his subjects by the method of adaptometry a sharply heightened sensitivity of the nervous system under the action of centimetric electromagnetic waves.[23] The most recent data on this problem may be found in a collection of experimental studies conducted under the direction of Professor A. V. Triumfov.[24]

---

[21] See V. Ya. Danilevsky, *Issledovania nad fiziologicheskim deystviem elektrichestva na rasstoyanii* (Investigations on the Physiological Effect across Distance of Electricity, Vol. I, Kharkov, 1900; Vol. II, Kharkov, 1901).

[22] See F. P. Petrov, Deystvie elektromagnitnovo polya nizkoy chastoty na vysshuyu nervnuyu deyatelnost" (The Effect of a Low-Frequency Electromagnetic Field on Higher Nervous Activity), *Trudy Instituta fiziologii imeni I. P. Pavlova,* I (1952), 369.

[23] See S. Ya. Turlygin, "O vozdeystvii santimetrovykh voln na tsentralnuyu nervnuyu sistemu" (On the Effect of Centimetric Waves on the Central Nervous System), *Doklady Akademii nauk, SSSR,* XVII, 1-2 (1937), p. 19.

[24] *O biologicheskom deystvii sverkhvysokochastotnovo elektromagnitnovo polya* (On the Biological Action of the Ultra-High-Frequency Electromagnetic Field), Sb. Leningrad, 1957.

Low- and high-frequency electromagnetic waves can act on the brain in the indicated manner only when their strength attains, as physiologists say, threshold magnitude; that is, that intensity at which the nervous processes, activated by them, can be perceived subjectively by man. The Soviet physicist, V. K. Arkadiev, turned his attention to this matter. On the basis of mathematical calculations, he came to the conclusion that the strength of these electromagnetic fields, generated by the biocurrents of the functioning brain, is very low and does not attain threshold magnitude. It is significantly less than the strength of the electromagnetic fields arising in the electrical apparatus and wires among which modern man lives and works. On that basis V. K. Arkadiev casts doubt on the electromagnetic hypothesis of the transmission of mental suggestion.[25]

The correctness of this hypothesis may be tested by still another method — that of the metallic screening of the mental suggester (the experimenter) or the percipient of the mental suggestion (the subject). In the Soviet Union the electrical engineer B. B. Kazhinsky was the first to apply this method. According to his data, metallic screening hinders the transmission of mental suggestion. The physicist, S. Ya. Turlygin, cited earlier, obtained the same result.[26]

It is to B. B. Kazhinsky's credit that he was the first one to try to answer the question of how the structural elements

---

[25] See his "ob elektromagnitnoy gipoteze peredachi myslennovo vnushenia" (On the Electromagnetic Hypothesis of the Transmission of Mental Suggestion), *Zhurnal prikladnoy fiziki,* I (1924), p. 215.

[26] See his "Izluchenie mikrovoln (λ=2mm.) organismom cheloveka" (Irradiation of Microwaves (λ=2mm.) by the Human Organism), *Byulleten eksperimentalnoy biologii i meditsiny,* XIV, 4 (1942), p. 63.

of nerve tissue may generate high-frequency electromagnetic waves. He points out that in electrotechnology such waves are obtainable by means of a closed, oscillating electric circuit of wires carrying alternating current, containing a condenser and solenoidal coils, and having some ohmic resistance. In the nervous system, the biocurrent which constitutes the basis of nervous excitation is an alternating current. Kazhinsky considers the ends of the dendrites, which look like disks, to be cellular condensers, and the coils of nervous fibers to be solenoids, included successively in a closed oscillating circuit; and he considers all of this to be a cellular vibrator generating electromagnetic waves of corresponding length.[27]

On the basis of these conjectures, the prominent histo-physiologist, Academician A. V. Leontovich, in collaboration with his son, an electrician, attempted to calculate theoretically the length of electromagnetic waves generated by the cellular vibrators of the brain, taking into account the magnitude of the electromotive force of the biocurrents, potential capacity of the cellular condensers, ohmic resistance of the nervous conductors, and the like. The results of such calculation coincided quite well with the diapason of cerebral radio wave-lengths determined in Cazzamalli's experiments.[28]

However, there are also contrary experimental data, indicating that shielding the inductor and percipient by iron or

---

[27] See B. B. Kazhinsky, *Peredacha mysley* (Thought Transmission), Moscow, 1923; *Biologicheskaya radiosvyaz* (Biological Radio Communication), Kiev, 1962.

[28] See the article by A. V. Leontovich in *Yubileyniy sbornik* (Jubilee Collection) of the Academy of Sciences, USSR, Vol. I, Ufa, 1944. (In Ukranian.)

lead rooms with walls from 1 to 3 millimeters thick did not hinder, or even perceptibly weaken, the transmission of the mental suggestion of sleep or awakening.[29] Such rooms do not admit short (centimetric and metric) electromagnetic waves and to a significant degree weaken long (kilometric) waves. If we may credit the information, already widespread, of the American experiments in mental suggestion said to have been carried out on board the submarine *Nautilus*, then one can add that neither the kilometric intervention of sea water nor the steel sheathing of a submarine constitutes a hindrance to the passage of that energy which effects mental suggestion.[30] This casts doubt on the correctness of the hypothesis of the electromagnetic nature of the phenomena of suggestion at a distance.

All that has been expounded in this chapter indicates that the results obtained so far in studies of the facts of mental suggestion and their explanation from the point of view of the electromagnetic effect of one brain on another lead to no final conclusion. But let us assume that in the future we shall succeed in showing that under certain favorable conditions — rarely met, however — one brain can become the broadcasting station of electromagnetic, or some other, still unknown, waves, and another brain can become the receiving station of these waves. Let us assume further that the waves picked up are capable of initiating in the cerebral cortex corresponding neuro-

---

[29] See monograph by L. L. Vasiliev, *Eksperimentalniye issledovania myslennovo vnushenia*, Leningrad State University, 1962. (English tr.: *Experiments in Mental Suggestion*, Hampshire, England: Institute for the Study of Mental Images, 1963 — Tr.)
[30] See the journal *Znanie — sila*, No. 12 (1960), p. 18.

psychic processes. The question comes up: Will this damage in some way the materialist outlook, the generally accepted propositions of physiological science? Not at all.[31] On the contrary, it opens a new sphere of facts for physiological investigation, and the sharp, shattering weapon of scientific materialist analysis will still serve to combat deep-rooted mystical notions.

---

[31] Professor V. P. Tugarinov, in his article "Yeshcho raz o peredache mysley" (More on Thought Transference), *Znanie — sila*, No. 7 (1961) p. 22, also acknowledges this.

What Can Be Said about "Extrasensory Perception?"

CHAPTER VII

What Can Be Said about "Extrasensory Perception?"

PARAPSYCHOLOGISTS THINK that in the process of evolution living beings, and in particular man, developed, for perception and the exercise of influence at a distance, organic adaptations that one can compare with modern achievements in radio technology and electronics. Thus, telepathy resembles communication which is effected by wireless or radio; telesthesia — television; telekinesis — telemechanics: that is, the control of various apparatus and processes at a distance by means of electronic equipment.

There is nothing absurd in this idea itself. One can adduce many examples confirming it.

The eye is constructed and functions approximately like a camera: the crystalline lens is a distinctive object glass, the layer of photo-sensitive cells in the retina (the rods and cones) is, so to speak, an organic photographic plate, and so on. Dolphins and some nocturnal animals (bats) possess organs for ultrasonic localization, and fish dwelling in muddy waters (the Nile garfish) possess organs for radio-localization.[1] In some cases, technology has surpassed by far what living beings had attained in the process of evolution. In other cases, however, man's inventiveness obviously lags behind the resources of organic nature. No chemical analysis of the atmosphere, for instance, can single out those smells which the noses of hunting dogs and of many wild animals detect and recognize.

Parasychologists seek to prove, by a number of special experiments and observations, that at least some animals and individual people are able to perceive objects and occurrences even under such conditions as to exclude, as it were, completely the possibility of perceiving them by the usual sense organs (by sight, sound, touch, smell): for instance, the ability to find out what is in sealed, opaque envelopes ("clairvoyance") or what is taking place at a very great distance ("far-sight"). In technology, röntgenoscopy corresponds to the first; television to the second.

Let us then acquaint ourselves with some of the phenomena that parapsychologists consider as existing and as demonstrating the reality of "extrasensory perception." One must put in first place the method, already known to the Greeks and Romans, of detecting underground water and ores with the aid of divining sticks appropriate to each.

The astonishing diversity of reactivity of the human organism, exhibited in such cases, was illustrated some years

----

[1] Now a new science, called bioelectronics or bionics, is concerned with these questions.

ago by the engineer N. A. Kashkarov, Professor at the Tomsk Institute of Technology, as follows:

"Holding in his hands a simple forked branch of a nut-tree, a man endowed with an aptitude for water-divination can, by the turnings of this branch (brought on by his reflex tremorous movements), point to the place where an underground stream may be found; can estimate its width, the approximate depth of the channel under the surface of the earth, and the direction of flow of the water, and can trace its course. Many water-diviners, if they are within the field of influence, sense the presence not only of streams of underground water, but also of gas pockets and electric currents, and, finally, they detect the presence of metal deposits and veins of ore. After prolonged training, some diviners develop the ability to distinguish the sensations elicited in them by various substances and to determine what is acting on them."[2]

The method of the water-divining stick is even now an important one, since it finds practical application in many countries.[3] It has an involved history, and an extensive literature is devoted to it; it has more than once been discussed at international scientific congresses. In 1913, for instance, a water-diviners' competition was conducted in Paris at the Second

---

[2] N. A. Kashkarov, *Obnaruzhenie podzemnykh vod po izmeneniam, vyzyvayemym imi v atmosfere* (Detection of Underground Waters by Atmospheric Changes They Effect), Kiev, 1916, pp. 5-6.

[3] In 1961 I received a letter from the Czechoslovakian water-diviner S. Dokulil, in which he, disputing a German professor who published a book on this question (O. Prokop, *Wunschelruthe, Erdstrahlen und Wissenschaft*, Berlin, 1957), writes that for thirty-two years he has successfully employed a water-divining stick at the behest of agricultural cooperatives.

Congress of Experimental Psychology. Many of the participating diviners were able to perform all the tasks scheduled in the program of stipulated experiments. These tasks corresponded to the kinds of divining enumerated by N. A. Kashkarov. The Congress acknowledged as demonstrated fact the ability of some people to detect water and ores by the stated method (by means of a wooden or metal stick), and proposed that further efforts be directed to the study of the physical force that causes in diviners the muscular reaction setting the stick into motion. Ch. Richet named this force — engendered by a spring which is underground, by gases which have collected in an underground cavern, or by a vein of metallic ore — *la force rhabdique*. In his opinion, it is a kind of "as yet unknown vibration" capable of enhancing a latent sensitivity of the human organism *(cryptesthésie)* — a sensitivity again unknown to the physiologists and psychologists. On this basis, Richet,[4] as well as Barrett,[5] assigned the given phenomena to the field of parapsychology, considering them as related to "clairvoyance."

Other authors (Chevreul, for example) saw in the movement of the water-divining stick something in common with ideomotor behavior, described in Chapter V. In their opinion, experienced diviners can discern the site of a spring or a vein of ore by the nature of the soil and vegetation, and the suggestion, arising this way in the mind of the diviner, is expressed by a corresponding movement of the stick.

---

[4] Ch. Richet, *Traité de metapsychique*, 2nd edn., Paris, 1923, p. 297.
[5] See W. Barrett, *Zagadochniye yavlenia chelovecheskoy psikhiki* (*Psychical Research*), Moscow, 1914.

Finally, physicists, busy with the question (the French-man Henri Mager,[6] for example), tried to understand the given phenomenon from a biophysical point of view and to replace the diviner and his stick with some physical instru-ment. The first attempt to construct such an instrument was made in 1903, by Schmidt in Berne. The presence of an underground stream was found through the oscillations of the weakly magnetized needle of this instrument.[7] This means that the mysterious *force rhabdique* is either electric or magnetic in nature.

Today more complex instruments and radio methods of prospecting the depths of the earth are applied. However, it must be acknowledged that cases have been reported in which physical instruments did not give reliable findings, while the water- or ore-diviner solved precisely the task set. According to Kashkarov's data, the diviner's organism is better than any existent physical instruments and reacts, moreover, to changes in ionization and to descending electric currents. These cur-rents are detectable over places where underground waters are flowing or where a vein of ore is to be found, and are attributed to increased discharge of the radioactive gas radon from the ground into the air.

The true reason for the diviner's motor reaction, whereby he predicts the presence of ores and springs, is not yet known for certain, but it looks as if we must turn to the biophysicists

---

[6] H. Mager, *Kak nakhodit istochniki i rudu s pomochyu orekhovoy ili metallicheskoy palochki i raznykh nauchnykh priborov* (How to Detect Springs and Ores by Means of Nut-tree or Metal Sticks and by Various Scientific Instruments), Kiev, 1913.

[7] For a description, see N. A. Kashkarov, op. cit.

for progress in the solution of this question. However, we do not know why only a few, rarely-met representatives of the human race possess the aptitude of water and ore divination. Such exclusiveness of possession is a characteristic of all parapsychological phenomena — a fact which greatly impedes their study.

There exists still another group of phenomena which, like water-divining, is designated by the term "clairvoyance." However, in contradistinction to water-divining, these phenomena are characterized by extraordinary (supernormal) acuity of the usual sense organs — sight and hearing. This has been observed in persons who have been hypnotized or who have sunk into autohypnosis, also known as trance.[8]

The annals of medical science record many cases of pathological sharpening of the senses. Dr. Brash, for example, tells of an apparently healthy man who suddenly noticed in himself an unusual acuity of vision: he clearly distinguished the smallest objects at a very great distance. Such a state lasted nearly 24 hours, then apoplexy developed, and the patient died; an autopsy disclosed a brain blood-clot of recent origin on the right side of the optic prominence. As Dr. Mitchell affirms, several of his neurotic patients were able to read when the light was so poor that normal people had difficulty in distinguishing even the largest objects.[9]

---

[8] The word "trance" is derived from the Latin *transire* — to cross over — and signifies the transition from a normal to "an unusual state of passivity, conscious or unconscious, physiological or pathological, during which the life of the brain slips from control by the will."

[9] See Dr. Beard's article in D. I. Mendeleev, *Material dlya suzhdenia o spiritisme* (Materials for the Appraisal of Spiritism), p. 287.

The sharpening of hearing in some hypnotized persons and hysterics can be so considerable that even the softest whisper can be heard by them at a great distance.

Sometimes the acuity of sight or hearing reaches such proportions as to be unbelievable. Here is one such case, communicated in a letter to me by Drs. Shilo and Lapitsky of the Polotsky Psychiatric Hospital. The case was that of a middle-aged intellectual suffering from alcoholism. During one of his regular hypnotherapeutic sessions, in the presence of the hospital personnel, the following occurrences were observed (Case History No. 186, 1957):

"A newspaper is picked from a great pile of newspapers and magazines on a bookstand and given to the patient with the command to read the name of the newspaper with his eyes shut. The patient is silent and does not open his eyes. Then the doctor draws the right index finger of the patient along the name of the newspaper, as if to direct his attention mentally to the given spatial area with the aid of the kinesthetic sense of the hand (without the finger touching the text). The patient correctly pronounces the name of the Byelorussian newspaper *Zvezda* [Star]. Then in the same way the patient reads headlines, single sentences, words in smaller type. Finally, with eyes shut, he reads the headlines in Pravda — first through a single sheet and then through double sheets of unlined blank paper. Upon awakening, he remembers that he saw the large print of the headlines as if "through a fog" and that the small print of the text "blurred in his eyes."

The experiment was first conducted under bright lights. When the lights were dimmed, reading became more difficult.

Also progressive thickening of the "paper barrier" (from one to three sheets) increased, correspondingly, the difficulty of reading. The possibility of a prior acquaintance with the newspapers on the part of the patient was completely excluded, since he did not have access to the room in which they were kept and he was not forewarned about the nature of the experiment."[10]

The authors of the communication recalled to me an analogous observation by one of the greatest Russian psychiatrists, S. S. Korsakov. One of his patients, a hysterical young girl, possessed the ability, "with the assistance of touch, of a general sense, of a special heat sensation," to read what was written on a sheet placed inside an envelope together with a photographic plate; to read through several layers of paper, and even to distinguish handwriting and the color of ink.[11] Professor Korsakov wrote apropros of this that "patients sometimes astound onlookers by telling them of things that could not be learned through the usual receptivity of the sense organs, and which appear to gullible people to be a manifestation almost supernatural."[12]

A similar experiment was performed in 1962 at the psychological laboratory of the Nizhni-Tagil Pedagogical Institute. It became the object of attention of the Scientific Conference of the Ural Division of the All-Union Society of

---

[10] Quoted with permission of the authors of the above communication.
[11] The photographic plate was put in as a check, in case the patient had attempted to look inside the sealed envelope (after the experiment, the photographic plate was developed).
[12] S. S. Korsakov, *Kurs psikhiatrii* (A Course in Psychiatry), 3rd edn. Moscow, 1913, I, pp. 95-96.

Psychologists meeting there. The conduct of these experiments was written up a number of times in the newspapers.

"They bound Roza Kuleshova's eyes with a kerchief. Nevertheless, by running the fingers of her right hand along the printed text, she continued to read a newspaper with ease. She was given a photograph; and again, though not seeing it, she determined with her fingers the pose and appearance of the person represented in the photograph. Paper slips of different colors were inserted into an envelope of opaque paper, and Kuleshova named the color of each. From a closed bag Kuleshova correctly took out skeins of thread of designated color or a specified playing card. She even determined by touch the subject of the tiny picture on a postage stamp.

"Roza herself gives the following explanation: when touching a colored surface, she perceives one color as wavy lines, another color as dots, a third color as crosses. Simultaneously, there arises in her mind a visual representation of the given color. This extraordinary sense of touch Kuleshova developed by persistent exercise. At one time she worked in a school for the blind. She developed rheumatic encephalitis, after which her touch became even more sensitive. In Roza appeared the ability to see color, as it were, by touch."[13] As further experiments showed, Roza can with her hand read a text on top of which is a celluloid film. Touching the object itself with her fingers was not a prerequisite for the success of the experiment.

---

[13] The newspapers: *Uralsky rabochy,* October 12, 1962; *Izvestia,* October 24, 1962, p. 6; *Smena,* December 15, 1962.

Scientists are at a loss to explain these surprising phenomena. One scientist holds that Kuleshova reacts to the subtlest differences in the temperature of the differently colored surfaces of objects; maybe this is why her touch is weaker in the dark. Another surmises that Roza senses with her fingers the structural differences of the dye. A third calls to mind in this connection the experiments of Professor A. N. Leontiev, who twenty years ago found a method of sensibilizing the skin of the palm (that is, of increasing its sensitivity) to enable it to "perceive" a pencil of light the heat of which was completely eliminated by special filters. Sensibilization of one part of the skin sets up electrical stimuli in another part, enabling the subject to know when the light operated on the skin and when it ceased to operate. The subject, securely blindfolded, not only sensed light with his skin but was also able to distinguish a red beam from a green.

I. P. Pavlov, probably, had similar instances in mind when, after describing the extremely fine differentiation of conditioned stimulations in experiments on the dog, he continued: "In us, in human beings, our higher conscious activity runs counter to these lower abilities to differentiate and hence hinders fine differentiation. That this is so is demonstrated by the fact that, in some instances, when man's normal conscious activity is altered, his ability to differentiate is sharpened. During special states of so-called clairvoyance, the differentiating ability in man reaches infinite sharpness."[14]

------

[14]I. P. Pavlov, *Lektsii po fiziologii* (Lectures in Physiology), Vol. V of his *Polnoe sobranie sochineniy* (Complete Collected Works) 1952, p. 520.

It is not reported whether, in the experiments cited above, the experimenter was familiar in advance with the objects perceived under controlled conditions by the subject. If there was pre-knowledge, then the results obtained in the experiments could be attributed to involuntary mental suggestion coming from the experimenter. To eliminate the possibility of such telepathic transmission, parapsychologists hand their subject an envelope whose content is not known to anyone present at the experiment. The sealed envelope with its unknown assignment enclosed (a drawing, for example, or a written sentence) is prepared beforehand by someone who is a stranger to the subject, who is not present at the experiment, and who does not know when and with whom the experiment will take place.

Parapsychological literature contains accounts of many experiments, conducted under controlled conditions, with persons endowed, presumably, with the gift of "clairvoyance." The most successful results were achieved with the Polish engineer Stefan Ossovetsky. In 1921 Professor Ch. Richet and his collaborators arrived in Warsaw from Paris for the sole purpose of conducting a series of experiments with him. Before the experiments, some of the collaborators or Parisian acquaintances of Richet had prepared some inscriptions and line drawings, put them into opaque envelopes, which were then sealed and turned over to Richet. Richet appeared on the experimental scene with these envelopes. Neither Richet himself nor any of those present knew what was contained in the envelopes. The envelopes were handed one after another to Ossovetsky. Crumpling each envelope in his hand, he quickly and nearly always precisely named what was in it.

For example, the parapsychologist, P. Sudre, had sealed a note in an envelope with a saying of Pascal's, "Man is only a reed, the weakest in nature, but this reed thinks."

Ossovetsky read: "From the thoughts of Pascal. Man is weak, he is a feeble reed, a reed the most thinking."

In another experiment Ossovetsky was handed a soldered lead tube containing a note. The subject's version of it was: "This is a drawing. A man with a big mustache and thick eyebrows. There is no nose. He's in military dress. He looks like Pilsudsky. This man is not afraid of anything, he is like a knight."

The drawing was extracted from the tube (whose sides were three centimeters thick) and was found to have corresponded exactly to the description given by Ossovetsky; the caption read: "Knight without fear and without reproach."[15]

Richet carried out eleven similar experiments during his stay in Warsaw, and all of them yielded approximately the same results as the two cited by us. Richet gave a high rating to the conclusiveness of these experiments. "We were convinced," he wrote, "that the surprising facts we had heard about Ossovetsky were in no way exaggerated." However, since we do not know all the details concerning the preparation and conduct of these experiments (they are too briefly described by Richet), we cannot unconditionally accept so crucial a

---

[15] These examples are drawn from Ch. Richet's treatise, *Traité de Métapsychique*, Paris, 1923, pp. 251-53.

conclusion.[16] We shall add to the above that Ossovetsky gave his demonstrations in a state of trance, which he was able to induce in himself by autosuggestion and dismissal of extraneous thoughts.

In 1946, Professor P. V. Terentiev (a statistical biologist), Professor Ya. I. Perikhanyants (a medical therapist), and I, carried out an analogous series of experiments, the organization and results of which I will let the reader himself judge.

A new scientific worker (a physiologist) consented to be a subject. She gave no signs whatsoever of possessing parapsychological capabilities. We therefore attempted to give rise to them by artificial means, employing an extract from the Mexican cactus peyotl with a high concentration of mescaline which greatly heightens the excitability of the cerebral cortex, especially the visual zone. Two hours after taking the extract, on closing her eyes, extraordinarily vivid and beautiful images, kaleidoscopically superseding each other, began to arise in the subject's field of vision, bringing her to an ecstatic and excited state. Experiments testing for extrasensory perception were conducted when this effect of peyotl was in full swing.

Various small objects, compactly wrapped in white absorbent cotton, were put into ten black plastic boxes (one object to a box) the tops of which were then screwed down. Nobody at the experiment knew what objects were placed in any of the boxes. During the experiment, the boxes were in an

---

[16] It should, however, be stated that in the course of many years Ossovetsky gave demonstrations (and always with success) before very many scientists of various disciplines, and not one of them was able to catch him in any fakery.

adjacent room. Taken at random, one of them was given to the subject who was asked to name, utilizing free-association, the images that came to her mind, and then to attempt to guess the object in the box. Everything said by the subject was taken down by a recorder. After each trial (there was a run of ten trials, one for each box), one of the experimenters went into an adjacent room, unscrewed the cover of the box, and through the door dictated to the recorder the identification number of the object disclosed (corresponding to a list of objects in his possession).

I cite the complete record for a run of trials undertaken on May 19, 1946, from 5:25 to 5:37 P.M. (see p. 163).

In our opinion the first of the ten trials is completely successful, while the fifth and eighth may be recognized as partly successful, especially since two control runs of trials with the same subject, undertaken a day before ingestion of peyotl and five days after its ingestion, produced no such results (they were noticeably worse).

The reader may consider that we are overrating the results obtained, and in his own way will be right in so thinking. An unavoidable defect of such experiments lies in their highly subjective evaluation, and it is hardly possible to eliminate this subjectiveness.

Therefore, modern parapsychologists prefer to use the method of quantitative analysis based on experiments using Zener's cards. The data, obtained in this way, easily lend themselves to statistical treatment, and objective evaluation.

This method, as applied to telepathy, was described in the preceding chapter. The method is also applied in experiments

TRIAL NUMBER	IDENTIFICA- TION NUMBER OF OBJECT	OBJECTS IN THE BOXES	THE SUBJECT'S ANSWERS
1	10	A one-ruble postage stamp depicting the Central Telegraph Building in Moscow.	A stone house. How did you contrive to hide a house in here?
2	6	Three branches of red coral.	A red stain.
3	4	A 1940 copper kopeck.	Whatever you wish: a column, a blue necklace, a knob.
4	5	A dried blossom of yellow mimosa.	A red patch of light. A green table, a round, soft table.
5	7	A small pendant compass.	Something that is yellow, oval, hard, orange and tinkles.
6	2	A vial of oil with a cork stopper.	Nothing there.
7	9	A fresh leaf of the spiderwort.[17]	Something long, a snake, a ring, blue. It's cold. That's enough!
8	8	A small frog (preserved in alcohol).	White cotton wadding, yes, cotton wadding, something alive.
9	3	An amethyst.	A small kerchief (the subject sings.)
10	1	An empty box with only cotton wadding.	A white shawl. Oh. I'm tired of this, someone lives there, a gentle man.

[17] An indoor grassy plant with long, falling, tangled, drooping creepers and leaves of oval form.

to detect "extrasensory perception," but with one difference: the experimenter does not look at the card he has pulled out, but merely holds it apart from the pack until the subject has written down his response and given the signal for the next trial. According to the data of Dr. Rhine and his followers, a large number of such runs, carried out on parapsychologically gifted subjects, sometimes yields results as improbable as those obtained in telepathic experiments, carried out with identical Zener's cards.

We shall not dwell here on cases taken by parapsychologists as "far-sight" since two such cases, reported by Richet, have already been cited at the end of Chapter II (see pp. 33-34).

We can now answer briefly the question posed in the title of this chapter. In the concept of "extra sensory perception" are lumped phenomena of various kinds and nature. Some of them have the character of motor reactions to "unsensed" (subsensory) influences of some kind of radiation from the ground — radium (radon) emanations, or local increased ionization of the air caused by the latter. Some persons are especially sensitive to the enumerated geophysical factors, while for the majority they remain below the threshold of sensitivity. Here, apparently, is nothing parapsychological, just as there is nothing parapsychological in the other group of phenomena characterized by a temporary supernormal increase in the sensitivity of vision, hearing, and so forth on the part of the usual analyzers. Finally, there is the third group of phenomena, accepted only by parapsychologists, which consists in the perception of things and events either through some kind of still unknown sense organs (Professor Richet's *cryptesthésie*) or directly through one set or another of neurons of the cerebral cortex, but by-passing the usual sense organs — something that in itself is quite difficult to imagine.

Paraphychologists are able to present less data for the existence of this last category of phenomena than for the existence of mental broadcasting. Nonetheless, the experiments of Richet, Rhine, and many others cannot simply be waved away. Further patient research is necessary. We declare: *Ignoramus sed non ignorabimus* (we do not know, but we will know)![18] It will not be out of the way to add that one of the most prominent biologists, I. I. Mechnikov, assumed the existence of "clairvoyance," considering it to be in man an atavistic trait transmitted from animals. "It can be," he wrote, "that some well established phenomena — 'clairvoyance' — may be reduced to the awakening of special sensations, atrophied in man, but present in animals."[19]

---

[18] A paraphrase of the well-known Latin aphorism of Du Bois-Reymond: "We do not know, and will not know!"

[19] *Etyudy optimisma* (Optimistic Sketches), Moscow, 1917, p. 188.

CHAPTER VIII

Is Transmission
of Muscular Power at a
Distance Possible?

CHAPTER VIII

Is Transmission of Muscular Power at a Distance Possible?

THE ACHIEVEMENTS OF TELEMECHANICS and the invention of radioelectronic apparatus for remote control of various machines and industrial processes automatically make us wonder whether the living organism does not also possess, in some measure and form, a capability of not only perceiving at a distance, under some conditions, but also of exerting an influence at a distance by means of a self-generated electromagnetic or as yet unknown energy. In Chapter V we have already mentioned the remarkable electrotechnical mechanism by means of which the electrical currents of a man's muscles put the fingers of a "mechanical hand" into motion even when he merely thinks of some movement. Mention was also made (in Chapter IV) of a low-frequency electromagnetic field (of the order of 40 to 50 cycles per second), produced by the electrical currents of the contracting muscles, which can be detected by a radio receiver tuned in on the same frequency.[1]

---

[1] One can now report in addition that recently (in 1960) the American physicists Volkers and Candib detected also high-frequency biocurrents (up to 150,000 cycles per second) of contracting muscles in man. These currents are very weak; nevertheless, they, too, have to generate radio signals of the same frequency around the functioning muscles.

In the near future we may expect to utilize at a distance instrumentally amplified radio waves originating from the muscles, heart, and brain in behalf of practical needs of one kind or another. But does there actually exist in nature itself, in the world of living creatures, any natural receivers of these waves?

Apparently, there does. Here is one of the examples pointing to their existence:

In 1928 there was published the unique study of Rudolf Reutler, director of a malaria laboratory at Rosh Pina (Palestine): *L'Action par distance des organismes vivants sur les organes vivants isoles*.[2] He investigated the peristaltically contracting internal organs of insects, in particular the digestive tract, the excretory system (the Malpighian tubes), and the sexual glands (ovaries) of the female Asiatic locust. These, when specially prepared and placed in physiological solution on a watch crystal, continue to contract rhythmically over a period of ten hours. Reutler noticed a sharp intensification of the contractions of these organs whenever he, while examining them through a binocular magnifier, strongly contracted the muscles (on sharp, deep inhalation): the intensification of muscles of his own hands, feet, or even of his respiratory peristalsis in the observed organs disappeared after the observer ceased contracting his own muscles. This remarkable phenomenon was noted by Reutler eighty times in his experiments on many prepared organs. The experiments were conducted under conditions of high room temperature (around 30°C) and the effect of the observer's warm exhalation on the preparation was

---

[2]*Revue mètapsychique*, No. 3 (1928) p. 197.

excluded. Reutler observed the same phenomenon even when, instead of human muscles, the muscles of insects near the preparation contracted (for example, the maxillary muscles of a preying spider eating his catch).

Thus, the functioning muscles of one living creature intensified the muscular contractions of another at a distance. This finding of Reutler's experiments gives an affirmative answer to the question posed by us, but it calls for confirmation. And that confirmation was supplied by the young entomologist, V. S. Steblin, at the Leningrad Institute of the Brain.[3] Following precisely the directions prescribed by Reutler, Steblin attempted to replicate his experiments on cockroaches — easily found in winter — and later on cockchafers. Out of ten experiments on cockroaches, intensification of peristalsis of the intestinal canal was clearly observed only in three instances where peristalsis was initially well expressed even without the muscles of the experimenter exerting any influence. V. S. Steblin attributes the absence of intensification of peristalsis in seven experiments out of ten to the imperfect conditions of his experiments (the comparatively low temperature in the laboratory and the depressed vital tonus (normal response to stimulation) of the insects taken for the experiments). And actually in experiments on newly caught cockchafers, given air temperature of 20-25°C, Reutler's phenome-

---

[3] Steblin died in 1942 during the siege of Leningrad, leaving his work unfinished. I cite his work from a preliminary communication to me, preserved in my files. Steblin's laboratory colleagues were also frequently present at his experiments.

non was observed with sufficient constancy. I offer an excerpt from Steblin's laboratory notes:

> "Contraction of the intestinal canal occurred at intervals of five to six seconds. Two or three seconds after the appearance of a peristaltic wave, when the intestinal canal is in a resting phase, the experimenter inhaled deeply. At the time of inhalation there was observed an out-of-phase wave of contraction of the upper part of the intestinal canal spreading further along the middle and lower intestinal canal. Three to four seconds later the experimenter made a forced exhalation, which as a rule was also accompanied by energetic contractions of the observed intestinal canal. The above described effect was invariably observed when the experimenter contracted the muscles of his upper and lower extremities." Malpighian tubes also reacted in a similar manner, contracting in a faster rhythm than the intestinal canal (one contraction every two to three seconds).

Whether any scientists abroad have replicated Reutler's experiments[4] I do not know, but can only cite the curious statement by an Englishman, Richmond, that he had succeeded in directing by mental power the irregular movements of paramecia (fresh water protozoa) to a predetermined area of the microscopic field of vision.[5] This statement has something in common with the quite incredible assertion by Dr. Rhine, who is already known to us, that it is possible by mental power to

---

[4]Reutler's phenomenon would be finally established and would have very great significance if one could succeed in registering it electrographically through leading off the biocurrents from the contracting intestinal canal to an oscillograph, equipped with an amplifier.

[5]*Journal of the Society for Psychical Research*, XXXIV (1952), p. 577.

control in some degree the fall of dice, making a die fall with that side up which was thought of. Rhine and his followers look on such facts as a simple manifestation of telekinesis (otherwise psychokinesis), that is, a manifestation of an ability, inherent in some people, to exert "by power of thought and will a direct mechanical influence on matter." Of course, for "thought or will," we may substitute the energy which, during their action, the brain, maybe, irradiates.

Let me describe the "dice-throwing machine" used in Rhine's laboratory. It consists of a reticulated cylinder, rotating around a central axis and set in motion by an electric motor. The experimenter sits on the right; on the left, the subject who is attempting to influence the die which will soon fall out of the apparatus. Under conditions of a like experiment minus any interference, pure chance has to direct the fall of the die, that is, with a sufficiently large number of trials each of the six sides of the die comes up the same number of times (the probability of occurrence for each side is equal to one-sixth). But if, as Rhine believes, a subject endowed with tele-kinetic ability will concentrate on one of the sides, for instance, on the side designated by the number 5 and ardently desires that just this side come up every time, then the effort, as it were, will not be in vain. The experiment will have outcomes beyond statistical expectation, that is, with a sufficiently large number of trials the side with the number 5 that was concentrated on will come up more frequently than is stipulated by probability theory. In another series of the same experiments the chosen side of the die was changed for every trial by lot;

for example, in correspondence to the page number of a book opened at random by the experimenter.

Parapsychologists have expended not a little effort and time in performing such experiments, but only several of them have succeeded in getting an outcome which deviates significantly from the number given by probability theory. Thus, in the experiments, for example, of R. H. Thouless, the chosen side of the die came up 2,809 times out of 16,232 trials, which makes a positive deviation of 104.[6] But the likelihood of obtaining such a deviation by pure chance occurs one time out of 33. Therefore, the findings obtained by Thouless are not very convincing, and those of several other investigators have in general been negative,[7] that is, they did not significantly deviate from the numbers given by probability theory.

In such cases materialistically-oriented parapsychologists (there are such) are repelled not only by the unconvincing character of the experimental findings, but also by the spiritualistic view of telekinesis as a clear manifestation of the "influence of spirit over matter," held by Rhine and his followers. Another view on this question, which postulates the existence of some physically operative material formation ("fluid," "ectoplasm") allegedly exuded from the human being who is endowed with the ability to produce telekinetic phenomena,

---

[6] For 16,232 trials the probable number of favorable outcomes for each of the six sides of the die is 2,705.

[7] These data are cited from the book of Robert Amadou, *La Parapsychologie*, pp. 274-82. Amadou himself, as are many other prominent parapsychologists, is skeptical about the results of these experiments. The existence of telekinesis is acknowledged by fewer modern parapsychologists than the existence of telesthesia, and especially, telepathy.

advances us no further. The reader who has carefully read through Chapter V will justly see in this a revival of mediumism, the trashiest variety of spiritualism. There is, however, one essential difference between parapsychologists and spiritists: spiritists ascribe the ability to produce telekinetic phenomena to "spirits," that is, to the souls of the dead, whereas several modern parapsychologists attribute these phenomena to the miraculous properties of the "spirit" or, at best, of the psychophysical organization of the medium himself.

Belief in the existence of persons endowed with telekinetic power is fostered not only by the laboratory studies of parapsychologists who have not lost hope of someday establishing indisputably the existence of this power, but also by the never-ceasing reports of everyday instances of its occurrence.

What, for instance, should we say about two such occurrences described in the autobiographical story by the respected Soviet writer, K. G. Paustovsky?

Recalling how difficult it was to get water in Odessa during the Civil War and how much it was therefore valued, the writer speaks about one unusual incident:

"We hauled water and poured it into a very large glass bottle in the corridor. One day Yasha Lifshits went into the corridor, and let out a wild scream. I rushed out of my room, and saw an inexplicable sight. Before our eyes the huge bottle began to tilt, remained for an instant or two in the attitude of the Leaning Tower of Pisa, then fell to the floor and flew into a thousand splinters. The precious water spilled over the staircase. We could, of course, have caught the bottle; instead we stood and looked at it, as if bewitched."

Paustovsky finds the second incident "even more amazing." Once, ill with the Spanish flu, he needed a thermometer, a great rarity at the time. After great difficulty one was procured from Academician Ovsyanniko-Kulikovsky. The patient's temperature was taken and the thermometer placed on the table. After this the patient fell asleep. And then the incredible happened:

"I was awakened by Yasha. He carefully opened the door. It creaked, and I awoke. I glanced at the table, and felt my hair stand on end — the thermometer suddenly began slowly to roll toward the edge of the table. I wanted to cry out, but the scene took my breath away. I saw Yasha's terrified eyes. He too was looking at the thermometer, and did not move. The thermometer slowly rolled to the edge of the table, fell on the floor, and smashed. My temperature dropped, evidently from terror. I immediately recovered."[8]

What would the spiritist, believing in "spirits," say about these curious incidents from the everyday observations of the writer, Paustovsky?[9] He would say that one of the witnesses of the described events, in all likelihood Yasha, was an unrecognized medium, an involuntary conductor of "spirits" to the material world, and that some playful "spirit" had used Yasha's mediumistic abilities to play a trick on him and his friend.

The modern parapsychologist, confident of the existence of telekinesis, would say something different: that one of the

---

[8] K. G. Paustovsky, *Povest o shizni* (The Story of My Life), Vol. III of his *Sobranie sochineniy* (Collected Works), Moscow, 1958, pp. 773-776.

[9] The author himself treats them somewhat humorously.

two was a powerful medium. But in another sense his organism, they would say, possessed the rare property of exuding some kind of energy or matter ("fluid," "ectoplasm"), which produced, at some distance from the medium himself, mechanical action.

Finally, a skeptic or even a plain sensible person would say: before making such speculative conjectures, let's see if Yasha himself could not have arranged all this, in order to play a trick on his friend. What will a person given to trickery, tomfoolery, and hoaxes not think up!

The great French mathematician Laplace very truly said: "We are so far from knowing all the forces of nature and the various modes of their action that it is not worthy of a philosopher to deny phenomena only because they are inexplicable in the present state of our knowledge. The harder it is to acknowledge the existence of phenomena, the more we are bound to investigate them with increasing care."[10]

The representatives of both the so-called exact sciences and the sciences studying the vegetable and animal kingdom should be guided by Laplace's golden words, which are obligatory also for the sciences studying man, his behavior, his personality, and normal and pathological psychic phenomena. They are obligatory, but, unfortunately, they are insufficient in application to the study of man and, in particular, to the study of his psyche.

Nature hides her secrets deep and far, but does not deceive or dupe the researcher. Man, however, can deceive.

---

[10] Pierre-Simon Laplace, *Essai philosophique sur le probabilité.*

Physicians, criminologists, psychologists, and especially parapsychologists, must always be on guard; intentionally or unintentionally they may be misled by patients, clients, and subjects — people who are often hysterical, psychically defective, and even twisted — with whom they are constantly obliged to work.

It is precisely in this category of people that celebrated telepathic percipients, "clairvoyants," and mediums frequently belong. The history of parapsychological research demonstrates convincingly that the most distinguished scientists have been severely deceived by the clever tricks of their subjects. Mathematicians, physicists, and chemists, accustomed in their scientific work to dealing with instruments rather than with human subjects, have been the victims of deception more commonly than physicians and physiologists.

D. I. Mendeleev was an unprejudiced investigator of parapsychological phenomena, but at the same time he also took into account in full measure all the dangers which lie in wait for the scientist in dealing with mediums and sensitives.[11] There were others abroad — Podmore, Lehmann, Beard, etc. As early as 1875, Beard listed a set of warnings which every parapsychologist should bear in mind even today. I let Beard speak for himself.

"Not to speak of the general subjective and objective precautions, necessary in every experimental investigation, we must, when studying the problem we are interested in [Beard is referring to hypnotism, which, at the time, seemed to be a

---

[11] On Mendeleev's struggle with spiritism, see Chapter V.

mysterious phenomenon], take additional measures for the elimination of the following special sources of errors: (1) intentional deception on the part of the subject; (2) unintentional deception on his part; (3) premeditated conspiracy by the participants in the experiment; (4) unpremeditated conspiracy by onlookers; (5) chance coincidences and guesses; (6) phenomena connected with involuntary movements and pathological states of the nervous system.

"All experiments with professional mediums and clairvoyants, carried out without taking into account and eliminating the enumerated sources of errors, have not the slightest importance for science and cannot be accepted as proof. Furthermore: if all the enumerated sources of errors were eliminated and the results of the experiments were improbable, then they too cannot be accepted, until they have been confirmed over and over again by experienced people."[12]

These precautions are taken by parapsychologists even now. They are of course wise, but they are sometimes excessive and become a drag on the further development of parapsychological research. For example, the English philosopher, George Price, is given to considering all parapsychological phenomena as in the category of the supernatural. Not so long ago he declared that he would be satisfied with just one positive parapsychological experiment, but one in which "an error or deception would be as impossible as the supernatural is impossible."[13]

---

[12] Beard, "Sushchnost i yavlenia transa" (The Essence and Manifestations of Trance), in D. I. Mendeleev, *Materialy dlya suzhdenia o spiritisme*, p. 296.

[13] G. Price, "Science and the Supernatural," *Science*, CXXII, 3165 (1955), p. 359.

The question then is: how can such a demand be met? Price has not been convinced by the statistical findings of Dr. Rhine and his school—findings whose data, provided by probability theory, scarcely involve the telepathic or tele-kinetic. He wants to see not "microparapsychological" phenom-ena, but at least one irrefutable "macroparapsychological," phenomenon. In my opinion the experiments on telekinesis carried out in 1930-1931 at the Paris Institute for Metapsychol-ogy by its director, Eugene Osty, in collaboration with his son, the engineer Marcel Osty, come close to meeting this demand.

In the previously cited Thouless experiments, the falling dice were presumably directed by telekinetic power, which did not require darkness for its manifestation. Osty's experiments, following the practice of usual spiritist séances, were carried out in darkness. There was also present a medium, a twenty-three-year-old Austrian, Rudi Schneider, who obtained fame for his telekinetic abilities. The only unusual aspect was the site for the séance—a laboratory filled with instruments, of whose purpose Rudi had not the slightest notion. These instru-ments, their configuration, and purpose are represented sche-matically in the figure on page 210 (top).

In the center of the room stood a little table; on it was put the object to be acted upon—usually a white pocket handkerchief. The medium was asked to move the object by means of his "telekinetic power," acting at a distance. With his back to the table, he sat down on a chair several meters away from it; all during the séance his hands and feet were held by inspectors, picked, in turn, from among the six to eight partici-pants in the experiment (co-workers at the Institute with E.

Osty at the head). In order to follow the medium's movements in the dark, bandages impregnated with a luminous phosphorescent substance were put on his neck, hands and feet. However, the principal inspection of the medium and the object to be acted upon was carried out by instruments and in quite a cunning way. An aperture in the ceiling above the table held an illuminator equipped with quartz lamps (14) radiating invisible ultraviolet rays. Underneath, the illuminator was tightly covered over by a screen (7) through which the ultraviolet rays could not penetrate (7); the screen was held in place by an electromagnet energized by electrical current from an accumulator (5). The same current also energized another electromagnet (11), which held closed the shutter of a camera (10) with quartz lens. The whole system of apparatus was controlled by other invisible rays — infrared. A beam of these rays was directed by a radiator (1) to the object to be acted upon (13), passed in its immediate vicinity on way to a tilted mirror (12), and, after reflection from it and passage over the object to be acted upon, entered an electric current which served to close the circuit (3).

Let us now imagine that Rudi, having managed to circumvent the vigilance of the inspectors holding him, reaches for the object (handkerchief) in order to move it from place.

In doing this, he would inescapably, if only for an instant, intercept with his hand (or some moving object) one of the beams of the infra-red rays, thus interrupting the circuit through which the current flows to the two electromagnets. Demagnetization would result, which in turn would release the screen of the illuminator and, simultaneously, the shutter of the camera. By the "invisible light" of the ultra violet rays, a photograph could be snapped of the medium, caught unawares and presumably exposed in his manipulation.

This is what was expected to happen. What did happen was quite different. The mechanical installation functioned properly throughout the séance. The photograph it produced, however, showed the medium in a pose of apparent innocence. Yet, seemingly without his agency, the handkerchief had been moved to the edge of the table, or tossed to the floor. How was this possible?

The answer suggested by the Ostys, father and son (in a monograph of 161 pages, with 61 illustrations[14]) is truly startling. Their evidence is that Rudi was in a deep trance; his appearance frightful. His rate of respiration had increased from the usual 12-16 per minute to 200-300 per minute. Nevertheless, he managed to articulate a few words, the purport of which was that a current of some invisible substance (la substance invisible) had exuded from his body; that Rudi could see this substance, and that furthermore he could control it, and through its agency shift the handkerchief.

The investigators decided to verify Rudi's claim through further experiment. They recorded galvanometric readings on a moving film, using a device (2) to which the galvanometer was attached, and which transformed the infra-red rays into electric current. The resulting record registered 70 electrograms, as shown in the illustration on page 210 (bottom).

---

[14]E. and M. Osty, "Les Pouvoirs inconnus de l'esprit sur la matière,' Revue métapsychique, No. 6, 1931; Nos. 1 and 2, 1932.

As this illustration may indicate, current is continuously passing through the galvanometer (upper curve): the lines below the curve represent the electromagnetic registration. Should the beam of the infra-red rays directed on the object be intercepted by the "invisible substance" that is being aimed at the same object, then the curve would make a sharp indentation in the form of a double tooth, indicating partial absorption of the rays. Thus it would appear to be possible to follow the "behavior" of the invisible substance through objective electrographic data.

Astonishingly, the data seemed to corroborate the medium's pretensions, both as to the flow of the "substance" and its effect on the object.

This is not all! Other details were no less striking. In its entirety, the experiment seemed to point to a discovery of paramount importance in the fields of physiology, psychology and even physics. What could this unseen agency be that could perform a mechanical task?

One might expect that publication of the results of the Osty experiments would have created a world-wide sensation, but nothing of the kind happened. The Ostys did not follow up their research, nor did anyone else check, confirm or try to refute its findings.

Some twenty years after the Osty experiment, Amadou, the French parapsychologist, in a published survey of parapsychology,[15] referred 23 times to various Osty studies and experi-

---

[15] Robert Amadou, *Le Parapsychologie: Essai historique et critique*, Paris, 1954.

ments, but he failed to utter one word about the monograph in question, as though it did not exist.

Thus, a strictly scientific approach to the "facts" concerning the transmission of muscular power through space permits us to conclude that we are here dealing with phenomena of a dual nature. On the one hand, we have a set of facts pointing to muscular activity of one organism linked with that of another, on the basis of which it is permissible to postulate the transmission through space from one animate being to another, as indicated also by the experiments of Reutler and Steblin. On the other hand, we have a set of facts on the basis of which is to be presumed the possibility of telekinetic influence on inanimate nature. However, the parapsychological experiments conducted for the purpose of proving the latter have either failed to exceed the fiducial limits of purely chance coincidence set by the theory of probability, or they do not exclude the possibility of errors on the part of the observer, or of fraud on the part of the subjects, to say nothing of self-deception owing to mental deficiency or abnormal personality. We must be careful indeed about experiments of this type, inasmuch as the unusualness and supernatural aspects of their findings foster the most absurd superstitions. All the more so, since a number of parapsychologists reinforce such superstitions with the weight of their scientific authority and by the semblance of strict empiricism in their research.

CHAPTER IX

Death and
the Superstitions
Associated with It

CHAPTER IX

Death and
the Superstitions
Associated with It

As ALREADY NOTED in Chapter I, belief in the existence of the soul after death was, and still is, the chief source of the anti-scientific fancies and superstitions prevalent among a vast number of people. But the time of the absolute dominion of blind faith has long since gone by. More and more people in this world prefer not to believe, but to know. Even the church itself has had to reckon with this and strives therefore to take over popular education, or in various ways to weed out (so far as that is possible) the atheistic content of the attainments of modern science and technology. The Roman Catholic Church organized its own universities to serve this end. Specifically, efforts are encouraged to "prove" scientifically (even experimentally) the existence of a soul in some form of supramaterial, supernatural manifestation, and its independence of all the laws of the objective world; the church, too, tries to be scientific about the possibility of the existence of the human soul after death; that is, the possibility of "personal immortality." There have been many such pseudo-scientific attempts; I shall cite a few examples only.

At the end of the last century two French hypnologists — first, A. de Rochas, in 1895, then P. Joire, in 1897 — informed the scientific world of a truly stunning "discovery" made by them: namely, the outward secretion (exteriorization) of dermal sensitivity. It has long been known that in deep hypnosis the skin loses its sensitivity to pain. In the opinion of these hypnologists, this manifestation allegedly takes place because the sensitivity to pain in the hypnotic is transferred from the skin to the surrounding air, forming a sensitive layer a distance of several centimeters from the surface of the body. When this layer is pricked sharply with a pin, the hypnotic screams, but in no way reacts when the pin is slowly and carefully passed through the layer and the skin itself is pierced. As the hypnosis deepens, the sensitive layer which has been formed allegedly moves increasingly away from the body and from it is formed a "fluid double" of the slumbering hypnotic — his ghost or phantom. This double can be seen by other hypnotics when the sensitivity of their visual organs has been heightened by verbal suggestion. But the experimenter himself is able to detect the location of the double only with the help of some sharp object, a needle, for example. When the double is pricked by the needle, the slumbering hypnotic screams and clutches at the corresponding part of his own body. In another book (1896) Rochas speaks of the possibility of exuding from the body of a hypnotic not only his sensitivity but also his muscular power, explaining thereby displacements of objects without contact, a phenomenon allegedly observed at mediumistic séances.

It is difficult to know what to ascribe all this phantasmagoria to — to the vivid imagination of the experimenters themselves, given to occultism; or to an unintentional suggestive influence exerted upon the hypnotic. Anyone who has worked with hypnotics of the somnambulistic type knows with what surprising ease they fulfill all the secret expectations of the hypnotist. His every gesture, intonation, a carelessly dropped word, are perceived by somnambulists as suggestion and result in corresponding effect (in the given case, the illusion of exudation from the body of a sensitive sphere, a self-generating psyche). A mistake in the conduct of a hypnotic experiment is taken for the truth and declared to be an experimental confirmation of what the experimenter expects to prove — the possibility of the existence of a soul, of a psyche beyond the limits of the physical body.

Another of Rochas's alleged discoveries had the same origin — his assertion that in very deep hypnosis one could revive and make manifest recollections of a previous incarnation of the soul: As when the hypnotic suddenly begins to speak in a voice that is not his own and in the name of some other person, who recounts his long-ago extinguished life. This is proffered as an experimental demonstration of the truth of the doctrine of reincarnation of souls.

However, aspirants to eternal life were most of all impressed with the "experiments" over many years of well-known scientists, headed by the prominent psychologist and father of philosophical pragmatisms, William James — all members of the London and American Societies for Psychical Research. These "experiments" had as their goal the conclusive demonstration that communication with the souls of the dead was possible by means of mediums allegedly capable of telepathically perceiving messages from the "other world", and transmitting these for general dissemination, by means of automatic writing.

The souls of the dead members of the above societies that "manifested" themselves in this manner tried to demonstrate their "identity" by recalling the most insignificant incidents of their life on earth.

Here, for example, is a sample of such a tragicomic conversation, between William James and his dead colleague Hodgson: "Do you recall, William, how, when visiting so-and-so in the country, we played such-and-such games with the children? Do you remember that when we were in such-and-such a room, furnished so and so, I said this and that to you?" "Certainly I remember, Hodgson." "Excellent proof, isn't it, William?" "Excellent, Hodgson." And so on, without end.

Even such an incorrigible mystic as Maeterlinck[1] was shocked by these conversations with the dead, and preferred to explain it all as the telepathic influence of William James himself, of his conscious or subconscious psyche on the automatically writing medium.

I have adduced these examples in order to show to what absurd lengths the persistent longing to convince themselves and others of the existence of the soul after death leads intelligent and educated people.

Even today some parapsychologists, especially in countries

---

[1] See his *Smert* (Death). Authorized (Russian) translation by I. Ardenin, St. Petersburg, 1914.

where religion still holds an important place in the minds of the people, cannot abandon the antiquated notion that some remnant of the human person presumably continues to exist after the death of the body, even if this existence is only temporarily, gradually dissipating. Scientists who wish to see in parapsychology a new branch of scientific knowledge are still forced to conduct a struggle with those who draw it to the bosom of religion, spiritism, and idealistic philosophy. One need only look through some of the recent issues of the *International Journal of Parapsychology*[2] to get an idea of what attention is given in it to questions of death and the existence of the person after death. Attempts are made to find arguments in behalf of the existence of their souls after death in the hallucinatory visions and last words of the dying. In this connection the monograph of the American parapsychologist Karlis Osis, *Deathbed Observations by Physicians and Nurses*[3] is typical.

The author of the monograph distributed 10,000 questionnaires to members of the medical profession, asking whether the dying exhibited an exalted mood, whether they saw apparitions and other hallucinatory visual images. Six hundred and forty completed questionnaires were received, on the basis of which the author arrives at the following conclusions: Fear of death is not the dominant feeling in the dying. Exaltation, an upsurge of exalted feelings, is more frequently observed. Hallucinatory visions whose content corresponds to traditional

---

[2]Parapsychology Foundation, New York.
[3]Parapsychology Foundation, New York. 1961.

religious beliefs are frequent. The hallucinatory appearance of ghosts of deceased ones, presumably assisting the patient to cross over to the after-death state, are especially frequent. It is observed, in addition, that such helpers are in the majority of instances the ghosts of deceased relatives of the patient. In all this, the author persistently emphasizes that these hallucinations and visions cannot be considered as the result of the action of medicines, a feverish state, or other pathological factors capable of causing hallucinations. On the contrary, such visions are experienced by patients when they are still fully conscious and reacting adequately to their surroundings.

Osis attempts to impart to his conclusions a pseudo-scientific appearance. But to an impartial reader of his monograph, there is obvious a concealed tendency to convince himself and others of the actuality of the existence after death of some remnants of the human person. This is no longer parapsychology, but a throwback to beliefs in spirits. Fortunately, a considerable number of parapsychologists abroad do not mix science with religion and take a negative view of a rapprochement of parapsychology with occultism and mysticism.

Physiology and medicine completely push aside spiritist gibberish, incontestably demonstrating that man's psychic activity ceases the very moment the organ of his psyche — the cerebrum — stops functioning.

For a sober scientific understanding of what death is, what precedes and what follows it, the remarkable achievements of a recently established branch of the medico-biological sciences, called thanatology (from the Greek *thanatos* — death) are of great importance. The noted Russian scientists Mechnikov,

Bakhmetiev, Kuliabko, Kravkov, Shor, and others have played a prominent role in the creation of this new science. One of the aims of this science is the study of those pathological processes which progress in a dying organism and lead to death (thanato-genesis), as well as the discovery of those methods which provide the possibility of staving off the dying of the organs most important to life, and, more than that, of even reestablish-ing their vital activity after they have already ceased to function (revival).

The causes that lead to the death of human beings and animals are varied: mechanical destruction of, or injury to, vitally important organs; their poisoning by toxic substances, introduced from without, or originating within the organism (toxins, bacteria, the toxic products of cellular distintegration, asphyxiation, loss of blood, etc.). But the dying period, called *agony*, sets in only after the indicated casual factors begin seriously to disturb the functioning of the two most important motors of life — the heart, which sustains the circulation of the blood, and the respiratory center, which gives rise to respiratory movements: inhalation and exhalation.

There exists a close mutual tie between the functioning of the heart and the respiratory center: the worse the heart begins to function, the more venous the blood becomes and the more the respiratory center is stimulated, which may lead to its over-excitation and paralysis. Conversely, the worse the respiratory center begins to function, the less the cardiac muscle receives oxygen and the more its functioning is disturbed. Complete cardiac failure rapidly entails interruption of the functioning of the respiratory center, and vice versa. In some cases the heart is the first to cease functioning; in others, the respiratory center. The result is death of the organism as a whole — clinical death, as physicians call it.

In the corpse, protected from the processes of decay, the life of its separate cells, tissues, and organs continues to glimmer for a long time. True death comes to the body's cells only after their inherent physiological functions have ceased finally and irreversibly. Prior to the arrival of this moment every dying cell passes through a unique state, which cannot be characterized as life (since its vital functions have already stopped) nor recognized as death (since, under certain conditions, its lost functions may be restored). The noted physiologist N. E. Vvedensky named this transitional, intermediate state between life and death *parabiosis*.[4]

The existence of a state of temporary suspension of all vital functions in some invertebrates (annulates, tardigrades, etc.) was discovered as early as the beginning of the eighteenth century. It was later named *anabiosis*. In the old book by Professor Halle, *Magic, or the Magical Powers of Nature*, already cited, one can read the following significant words: "It appears that in the nature of animals there is found a middle state, which is neither life nor death, but a middle existence, which may be called death-life." And further: "Mock death may be the best means against real death in men: for the mock dead cannot starve or suffocate inasmuch as life is possible without food or air."

The same book relates the first attempts at revival of higher warm-blooded animals. "In the presence of several

---

[4]In 1901.

witnesses, Professor Herward of Oxford opened a hound's vein and let out all its blood, so that there remained in it not even small indications of life (using the test of holding a mirror over its mouth), then he opened the vein of a prepared calf and by a clever device conducted its blood into the open vein of the dog. As the calf's strength waned, that of the dog revived, so that within a few hours it again took to eating. Later, when the dog was again used for the chase, no changes in its natural attributes because of the calf's blood could be detected."

At that time Peter I sent the first Russian physiologist, Piotr Posnikov, to the famed University of Padua. There, as contemporaries put it, he learned "to put to death live dogs, and restore life to dead dogs." In 1848, Professor A. Filomafitsky, of the University of Moscow, viewed blood transfusion as the only means of saving waning life. Systematic work on the problem of reviving higher animals was initiated in 1874, when the physiologist, Schiff, proposed the application of cardiac massage by means of its rhythmic compression, and the pharmacologist, Bem, of the Derptsky University began experimentation on the revival of animals after their fatal poisoning with chloroform and asphyxiation.

The first partially successful attempt to restore brain functions was made at the end of the last century, by the French scientist, Broun-Sekar, in experiments with the severed head of an animal (a dog). When it is deprived of the flow of blood, the brain immediately loses its functions. If fresh blood is forced through the vessels of the brain a few minutes after severance of the head from the body — this method is called perfusion — the brain reestablishes some of its functions: the ears stir, the eyes move, blink, and the pupils again react to light.

Later, the physiologists, Heymans, and Bukert confirmed and broadened Broun-Sekar's observations. It was found that the cerebral cortex is especially sensitive to interruption of the circulation of blood. Eight or ten minutes after severance of the head reestablishment of its normal activity is usually impossible. This interval of eight to ten minutes it sufficient for the originally reversible parabiotic state in the cortical nerve cells to go over to an irreversible state of biological death.

Other divisions of the brain are more stable, their transitional parabiotic state continues much longer. Thus, it may still be possible to restore the activity of the respiratory center, located in the medulla oblongata, by forcing blood or physiological solution, saturated with oxygen and warmed to body temperature (32° C), through the vessels of the brain twenty to thirty minutes after this center has stopped functioning.

The second motor of life — the heart — dies even more slowly. At the beginning of this century Professor A. A. Kuliabko carried out the following experiment: hearts of a rabbit, a cat, and even a human being were extracted from the organism immediately after clinical death and refrigerated for several hours. Nevertheless, they renewed pulsation on perfusion through the system of coronary vessels of physiological solution, warmed and saturated with oxygen, and continued to function for two to three hours afterward. Let us remember that the coronary vessels supply blood to the tissues of the heart itself, in particular the cardiac muscle.

This experiment demonstrated that the transitional parabiotic state in a dying heart lasts considerably longer than in a respiratory center that has stopped functioning. Of the three most important vital functions, it is easiest of all to restore cardiac function, more difficult to restore respiratory movements, and still more difficult to bring back higher nervous activity, without which reinstatement of man's psyche, his spiritual individuality, is impossible.

An important stage in the development of methods for revival of not only animals but also human beings was the experiments of F. A. Andreyev. In 1913 he devised a new method for restoring the activity of stilled hearts of exsanguinated or poisoned dogs. The method consists basically of a centripetal forcing (that is, a forcing in the direction of the heart) of blood into some major artery — either natural or artificial blood (Ringer-Lock's fluid) with the addition to it of adrenalin, a substance which stimulates cardiac activity. With such introduction of the revivifying fluid, the adrenalin easily enters the coronary vessels of the heart, which supply the cardiac muscle with blood.

It is safe to say that today the revival of higher animals, after an interval of time of not more than six to eight minutes after onset of clinical death, can be considered a fully demonstrated fact. This is, of course, possible only in those cases where death comes without destruction or anatomical injury to vitally important organs.

Here, by way of example, are the results of an experiment in reviving a cat that was brought to a state of clinical death by blood-letting. The experiment was carried out by I. N. Yanvareva in the thanatological laboratory of the Department of Physiology[5] at Leningrad University (see illustration on p. 207).

Heparin, a substance which prevents coagulation of the blood, was injected into a cat before the experiment. The animal was under light ether-chloroform narcosis; respiration was normal: blood pressure around 160 millimeters of mercury. Blood-letting from a severed artery was begun at 11:25 A.M. Within 2-3 minutes the blood pressure, by which cardiac activity is judged, dropped to 3-4 millimeters of mercury; the heart stopped, the ocular corneal reflex disappeared, respiration become intermittent; then came the final agonal breaths, and at 11:32½ (seven and a half minutes after commencement of blood-letting) clinical death came. At 11:37½ (that is, five minutes after the onset of clinical death) measures for revival were begun. Blood, let earlier from the same cat, warmed, and saturated with oxygen, was forced centripetally into an artery (following Andreyev's method); simultaneously, artificial respiration was applied by means of a special apparatus, and adrenalin, which stimulates heart action, was also injected.

As may be seen in illustration b, blood pressure immediately began to rise and after a minute and a half had already attained its original level. Thirty to forty seconds later, heart action had already been renewed. Independent respiration was

---

[5]See I. N. Yanvareva, "Izmenenie elektricheskoy aktivnosti prodolgovatovo mozga i bolshikh polushariy v period umirania, klinicheskoy smerti i ozhivlenia zhivotnykh" (Alteration of Electrical Activity of the Medulla Oblongata and the Cerebrum in the Period of Dying, Clinical Death, and Revival of Animals), *Vestnik LGU,* No. 9, Issue 2 (1959), p. 87.

still absent during this time. Only after 14 minutes, against a background of prolonged artificial respiration, did infrequent independent breaths of the agonal type begin to be observed. (See illustration B.) With their appearance the process of revival went faster; the ocular reflexes — the pupillary and the corneal — were restored; then the spinal defensive reflex (in response to pinching the paw). The central nervous system gradually reestablished its activity.

On page 208 are four drawings of the same experimental cat: before the experiment (A); an hour and a half after clinical death, which lasted five minutes (*b*); twenty-four hours after revival (B); on the fifth day following revival (*r*) — the animal has completely recovered from its clinical death.

The illustrations on page 209 show what happens to the cat's cerebral cortex at the time of dying from loss of blood (A), in the period of clinical death (*b*), and at the time just after revival (B). In these experiments a needle-like steel electrode, whose point touches the surface of the brain, is earlier implanted into some part or other of the skull (in the given experiment, the part corresponding to the motor cortical zone); another electrode is, prior to the experiment, attached to the ear of the animal. The implanted electrode transmits the electric potentials of the cerebral cortex through an amplifier to a cathode oscillograph. In this way the earlier noted electroencephalogram (abbreviated EEG) is registered on the photographic film of the apparatus.

The excerpt *a* in the illustration *A* shows the EEG of the cat prior to blood-letting; the animal is under light narcosis; blood pressure is around 140 millimeters of mercury; the EEG is normal in form. Excerpt *б* was recorded 15 seconds after blood-letting began; there are observable amplification and quickening of the oscillations of the electric potential, pointing to a temporary heightening of cortical activity; to its exaltation. Excerpt *б*, recorded one minute and 45 seconds later, shows the cortical depression that is already under way: the oscillatory rhythm has slowed down, infrequent sharp oscillations appear, which are considered a true index of depression. The blood pressure has already fallen to 4 millimeters of mercury, the ocular reflexes have disappeared. Excerpt *г* was recorded 4 minutes and 37 seconds after blood-letting began: the oscillations of potential begin to weaken intermittently; respiration stops intermittently; agony begins. Excerpt *д* was recorded after 7 minutes and 37 seconds: the oscillations of potential take on the character of isolated bursts (the so-called spindles), separated by long intervals; respiratory movements acquired the same character. Agony is in full swing; a few more final breaths, then clinical death comes.

In the illustration (*b*) that follows, one can trace how the final, barely perceptible, oscillations of cortical potential gradually reduce to zero (excerpts *a* and *б*).

The last illustration (B) shows the electroencephalograms recorded at various intervals after the process of revival had begun. The heart has already started to function a little after 30 to 35 seconds. In the upper excerpt *a*, recorded after 1 minute and 33 seconds, and even more distinctly in the following excerpt *б*, recorded after 2 minutes and 13 seconds, the rhythmic oscillations of the potential are registered; however, their rhythm corresponds to that of the heart's contractions. They are not as yet oscillations of the potential of the brain itself, but rather action. currents of a heart that has already begun to function — currents picked up from the surface of the cortex. Oscillations of the potential of the brain itself, as yet weakly expressed, appeared only after 13 minutes and 14 seconds (excerpt *б*). By that time occasional respiratory movements of the agonal type had recommenced. In excerpt *г*, recorded after 26 minutes and 9 seconds, we see an already dense series of oscillations of brain potentials. The ocular and spinal reflexes, evoked by pinching the paw, have been restored. In excerpt *д*, recorded 33 minutes and 20 seconds after revival began, the oscillations of potential are intensified even in comparison with the initial level, indicating a state of some exaltation in the restored cerebral cortex. Blood pressure stands at 115 millimeters of mercury; independent respiratory movements at 17 per minute. The cat will live!

This victory over death gained by scientists has great theoretical and practical importance. It is important theoretically for the following reasons: if a brain that has stopped functioning can be reanimated by the application of blood or a saline solution, this fact alone refutes the unscientific, metaphysical theory that the vital activity of the brain and the entire organism is generated by some unknown "vital force." Furthermore, if the organ of the psyche ceases to function immediately after stoppage of the heart and breathing, this means that the soul, which is tied to cerebral activity — that is, man's psychic life — cannot in any way exist after the death of the body. On the contrary, success has been achieved in demonstrating the possibility of temporary bodily vital activity with complete exclusion of the brain (the brain was already dead). This means that there has been demonstrated the possibility of bodily life with complete exclusion of psychic activity.

For example: even if perfusion of blood or a revivifying solution through the bodily vessels was started too late — at the expiration of 10-15 minutes after onset of clinical death — breathing and heart activity were nevertheless resumed, but the brain no longer reestablished its functioning. The animal remained in a state of deep coma and sustained muscular rigidity, then died finally 10-20 hours after the start of the experiment.

The practical importance of investigations of this type was demonstrated during the grim years of the Patriotic War.[6] Professor V. A. Negovsky and his co-workers managed in more than 50 instances to revive wounded soldiers who were dying from traumatic shock or loss of blood. True, some, nevertheless, as a consequence of irreparable injury to vitally important organs, died several hours or days after artificial revival; but the rest, literally, were snatched from the clutches of death. Here is at least one of these remarkable cases.

A soldier, Ch-v, was brought to a front-line hospital two hours after wounding of the right thigh. A few minutes after he was operated on, the surgeon certified death from shock and acute loss of blood: no pulse was felt, the heart stopped beating, breathing ceased, the pupils were maximally

---

[6]A Soviet euphemism for World War II — Tr.

dilated, all reflexes vanished, and the muscles of the body were completely flaccid. Clinical death had come.

Three and a half minutes later, Professor Negovsky applied his method: forcing blood simultaneously into an artery and vein to the accompaniment of artificial respiration. One minute after this, cardiac function was already restored; after three minutes independent respiration returned; after twenty-two minutes the brain began to revive — the ocular reflexes appeared; and after sixty minutes the first signs of restored consciousness appeared. After twenty-four hours the soldier, resurrected from the dead, was already able to read a book. Later on he recovered completely.

The method employing perfusion of fresh blood may be applied also in several other cases involving death: to people who have drowned, who have been burned, who have died from electric shock. However, as was to be expected, the human brain has proved to be still more sensitive to interruption of circulation of the blood and respiration than the canine brain.[7]

The period of transitional state — parabiosis — for the organs of the psyche in man lasts only 5-6 minutes. Up to expiration of this interval of time, it is still possible to restore the vital activity of the cerebral cortex, and with it, also its psychic activity. At the expiration of this critical interval of

[7]For more detailed information, see V. A. Negovsky, *Patofiziologia i terapia agonii i klinicheskoy smerti* (The Pathophysiology and Therapy of Agony and Clinical Death), Moscow Medgiz, 1954. Quite recently Professor Negovsky determined that by hypothermy, that is, by the gradual cooling of the body of an experimental dog to 26° — 29°C, it is possible to prolong considerably the period of clinical death (up to sixty or more minutes) with subsequent revival.

time, the brain, the psyche, the consciousness of man irretrievably perish. This is an immutable law of nature. Every sensible person should understand this, and once and for all dismiss all illusions of an existence after death.

Let us remember the poet's words, replete with human dignity: "I was, I am, I do not need eternity!"

Nor should we forget the sage advice of the great fighter against "scientific" superstitions, D. I. Mendeleev. He said that to wage a successful battle against idealism and mysticism one must study, patiently and at the same time boldly, all the neuropsychic phenomena that engender religious beliefs and all kinds of prejudices and superstitions. "We should not ignore these phenomena," he wrote, "but rather examine them carefully; that is find out what in them belongs to the field of universally known natural phenomena, what to fancy and hallucinations, and what to shameless fraud; and, finally, whether there is not something which belongs to the category of still inexplicable phenomena conforming to as yet unknown laws of nature. Such an examination will remove from these phenomena the seal of mystery which attracts many to them, and will leave no room for mysticism.[8]"

In writing this book, I have been guided by these wise words which warn against bias and a priori negativism, yet at the same time demand vigilant circumspection and a strict critical attitude.

---

[8]From Mendeleev's "Proposal" to the St. Petersburg University Physical Society for the establishment of a commission for the examination of phenomena called mediumistic (May 6, 1875). (See Mendeleev, *Materialy dlya suzhdenia o spiritisme*, p. 3.)

Illustrations

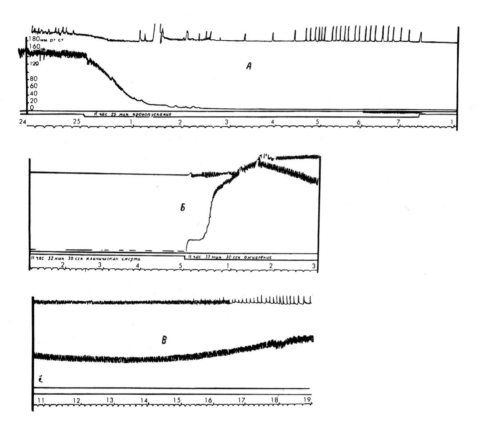

A. Death of cat, induced by bloodletting. Top — transcription of respirations; Center — transcription of blood pressure; Bottom — duration of time, recorded at intervals of twelve seconds.

6. Period of clinical death and beginning of resuscitation.

B. Further progress of resuscitation. Appearance of autonomous respirations.

Cat brought to a state of clinical death, then
resuscitated by the Andreev-Negovsky method.

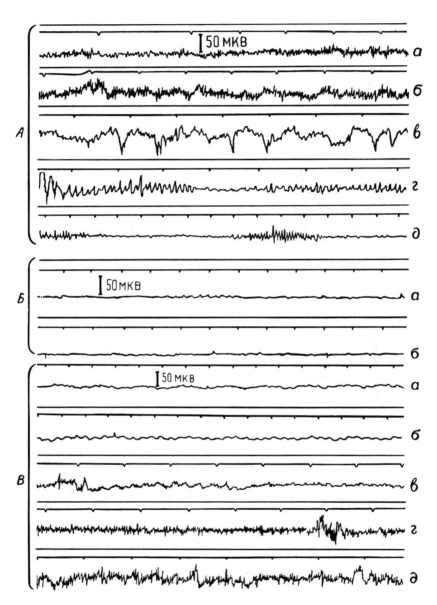

Electroencephalogram of cat during period of dying from loss of blood *(A);* At time of clinical death *(б)*; and during progress of restored cortical activity of the cerebral hemispheres and resuscitation, (B). Duration of time is marked in seconds. MKB (microvolts) denotes the scale of the biopotential's oscillations. Explanation in text.

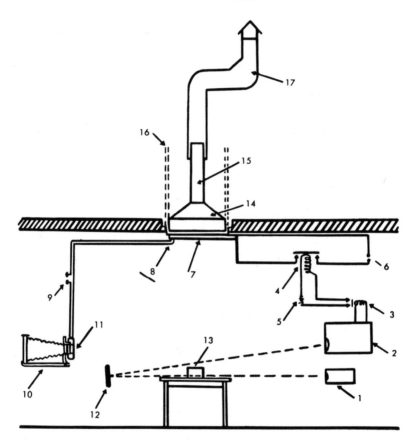

Top: Set-up for telekenetic experiments conducted in the laboratory of the Paris Institute of Metapsychology.

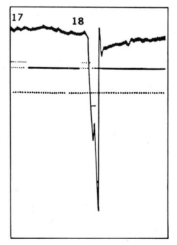

Bottom: Electrogram recorded by Dr. Osty during experiments with the celebrated subject R. Schneider.

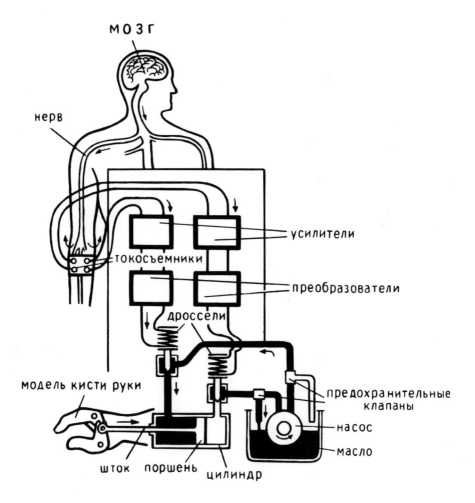

Dr. Vasiliev's caption describes this as an iron hand controlled by the biocurrents of the human hand's muscles. Which muscles? According to the text, the iron hand replaces a lost hand, so that Dr. Vasiliev's claim can only mean that the biocurrents of the brain, which formerly controlled the human hand's muscles, now control the iron hand. Competent medical authority describes the diagram as neither clear nor convincing. *Editor, English edition.*

Index

Academy of Sciences, Belgian, 83;
French, 50
Acuity of sense organs,
supernormal, 154ff, 164
Aesculapius, 48
Afterdeath existence, *see* Death
All-Union Society of
Psychologists, Ural
Division, 156
Amadou, Robert, 7n, 174n, 183
America(n), *see* United States
Amnesia, posthypnotic, 79
Anabiosis, *see* Parabiosis
Andreyev, F. A., 197, 198
Animal magnetism, 8, 49-52. *See
also* Hypnotism
Animals: hypnotization of, *see*
Hypnotism; revival of, 197ff.
See also Dogs
Animism, 11, 25, 115
Anokhin, P. K., 19
Arkadiev, V. K., 142
Artemidorus, 12
Asia, 120
Asiatic locusts, Reutler's
experiments with, *see* Reutler
Austerlitz, battle of, 68
Astvatsaturov, M. I., 14, 32
Autohypnosis, 154; of yogis, 40-1.
See also Hypnosis; Trance
Automatic: movements, 101-16;
writing, 111, 190. *See also*
Ideomotor activity
Autosuggestion, 50, 95, 98;
formula of, 97; during waking
state, 83-98. *See also*
Autohypnosis; Hypnosis;
Suggestion
Ayrapetyants, E. Sh., 31n

Bakhmetiev, 193
Balzac (Honoré de), 68
Barrett, William, 7n, 120, 152
Beard, Dr., 112, 154n, 178-79
Bekhterev, V. M., 14, 28, 31, 55,
63, 77-79, 85-86, 89, 90n, 91-92,
93n, 97, 116; Institute of the
Brain, 139
Belitsky, G. Yu., 114n
Bell (English physiologist), 42
Bem (pharmacologist), 195
Berne, 153
Berner (German psychologist), 16
Bernheim, 55, 57, 63
Binet, A., 73
Bioelectric currents: in brain, see
"Brain Broadcasting"; in
muscles, 109-10, 169ff
Bioelectronics/bionics, 150n
Birman, B. N., 22, 23n, 23, 60
Bloch, Bruno, 90-91
Braid (James), 39n, 53-54, 57, 102
Brain, the, physiology of, 15, 17ff,
and *passim;* functioning of, dur-
ing sleep, 16ff; electromagnetic
waves in, 136ff. *See also* Pavlov
"Brain broadcasting," 116-45, 165.
See also Telepathy; Transmis-
sion of Thought
Brash, Dr., 154
Breslau, 56
British Association of Scientists,
120
Bronshtein, A. I., 114n
Broun-Sekar, 195, 196
Brown, 112
Brownie, house *(domovoy)*, 44
Bruck, C., 131
Brugmans, Dr., 135-36

Bubnov, 56
Buddhists, and autosuggestion, 95, 98. *See also* Yogis
Bul, P. I., 58n
Burakovsky, V., 42
Burdach, K., 28
Bukert (physiologist), 196
"Burial alive," 37ff. *See also* Catalepsy
Bykov, K. M., 17, 31n

Candib (American physicist), 169n
Carpenter, Dr., 102
Cat, revival of, 197ff
Catalepsy/cataleptics, 37ff, 65
Cataleptic bridge, 64
Cazzamali, experiments of, in electromagnetic brain waves, 137ff, 140, 143
Cerebral cortex, *see* Brain
Charcot, 54, 55, 57, 62-63
Chermak, 42
Chevreul (Marie-Eugéne), 102, 103n, 152
Chicago, University of, 15n
Chicken, hypnotized, 49
Chistian zealots, and autosuggestion, 95ff
Christ's Passion, 83
Church the, *see* Religion; Roman Catholic, 187
Ch-v (soldier), revival of, 202-03
Civil War (Russian), 175
Clairvoyance/far-sight, 6, 12, 150, 152ff, 161-3, 178, 179, and *passim;* cases of, 32-33; water- and ore-divining as, 150ff, 152, 165. *See also* Acuity of sense organs, supernormal; telesthesia
Commission: for investigation of animal magnetism, 50-51; for investigation of mediumistic phenomena, 106-07
Conditioned reflex, *see* Pavlov

Congress of Experimental Psychology, First, 68; Second, 152
Coué, Emile, 97-98
Crookes, William, 7n
cryptesthésie, 152, 164
crystallomancy, 70

Daldis, 12
Danilevsky, V. Ya., 141
Death: cataleptic/mock, 37ff, 65, 194ff; existence after, 187ff; and reincarnation, 7-8, 189; and revival, 197ff; study of (thanatology), 8, 192ff; superstitions associated with, 7, 187-204
Delage (Yves), 26
Demons, belief in, 67
Derptsky University, 195
Deslon, 50
Dice, falling, experiments with, 172-74, 180
Disinhibition, *see* Excitation and inhibition
Divining underground water and ores, 150ff
Dog(s); Pavlov's and Birman's experiments with, 22-23, 60n; revival of, 195
Dokulil, S., 151n
Dominant, the, theory of, 76-79, 95, 98
Domovoy, see Brownie
Dostoyevsky, Fyodor, 47
Dream books, 12
Dreams, 11-33; creative, 28; diagnostic significance of, 16ff, 29, 32; falling, 28; flying, 27-28; Freud's theory of, 30-31; and hallucinations, 69-70; interpretation of, 12-13; Pavlov's theory of, 23ff; prophetic, 29; "telepathic," 32ff; "telesthetic," 32ff
Du Bois-Reymond (Emile), 165n

"ectoplasm," 174, 176
Egypt, 48
Eisemann, Dr., 88
Electroencephalography, 137, 138n
Electromagnetic brain waves, 136ff; Cazzamali's experiments in, 137ff, 140, 143
Engels, Friedrich, 5, 107
England/English, 7n, 127, 136, and *passim*
Epidemics, psychic, 85-86
Excitation and inhibition of cortical cells, 17ff, 76ff, 109, and *passim;* theory of the dominant concerning, 76ff
Existence after death, 187ff. *See also* Spiritism
Extrasensory perception (ESP), 6, 149-65. *See also* Clairvoyance; Telekinesis; Telepathy; Telesthesia
Exorcism, 88-89
Exteriorization of dermal sensitivity, in hypnotics, 188-89

Fakirs, Indian, 64, 126
Faraday, 102, 104, 120, 138
Faria, abbot, 53
Far-sight, *see* Clairvoyance
Feldman, O. I., 112n
Felida, case of, 45-46, 73
Ferraus, 90
Filomafitsky, 195
Fisher, F. F., 90n
Flammarion, C., 123n
Flaubert (Gustave), 68
Fludd (Robert), 49
"Fluid:" ectoplasmic, 174, 176; animal-magnetic, 49-52
"Fluid double," 188
Force rhabdique, la, 152, 153
Fortune-telling, 70, 103-04
Fox family, 101-02
Franklin (Benjamin), 50
Freud, Sigmund, 30-31

Galperin, S. I., 40n
Galvas, E. T., 72n
Gesner, K., 17
Gilbert, Dr., 33
Gnostic papyrus, 48
Goethe, 68
Gorkom, 121
Greece/Greeks, 48, 150
Groningen, University of, 135
Gurney, E., 123n

Halle, G., 38, 194
Hallucinations, 6, 65ff, 78; and dreams, 69-70; "negative," 78; "physiological," 68
Hand, mechanical, 109-10, 169
Hansen (hypnotist), 56
Havre, 33
Heidenhain, R., 55-56
Herward, Prof., 195
Hertz, H., 136
Heymans (physiologist), 196
Hodgson, 190
Holland, 136
House brownie, *see* Brownie
Huxley (Julian), 107
Hydromancy, 70
Hyperesthesia, 62
Hypnology, 55
Hypnotism/hypnosis/hypnotization, 5, 37-79, 178, and *passim*; of animals, 48, 58, 63, 65; Bekhterev's use of, as therapy, 92; cataleptic type of, 63; of cataleptics, 65; history of, 48-56; and hallucinations, 65ff; and illusions, 65; insensitivity to pain during, 188-89; of lethargics, 65; of somnabulists, 65, 72-74; and suggestion, 37-79; treatment of warts by, 90-91
Hypothermy, 42, 203n
Hysteria, 5, 45, and *passim*

Idealism, 7
Illusions, 65

Ideomotor activity/acts/behavior: in "mind-reading"/muscle-reading," 112ff; in spiritism, 102ff; Vasiliev's experiment in, 113-14, 144n; in water- and ore-divining, 152. *See also* Automatic movements
Indians, Mexican, 70
Inhibition, and excitation, *see* Excitation
Inquisition, Spanish, 4
Insensitivity to pain: in hypnotics, 188-89; induced by autosuggestion, 93-94
Institute of the Brain, V. M. Bekhterev, 139
Institute for Metapsychology, Paris, 180

Jacobson, E., 109n
James, William, 7n, 189-90
Janet (Pierre), 33
"Jesus-prayer," 95-97
Joire, P., 188

Kardanus, 12
Kartamyshev, A. I., 91n
Kashkarov, N. A., 151, 152
Kazhinsky, B. B., 142-43
Kherumian, R., 7n
Kircher, 49
Kobrinsky, A. E., 110n
Konstantinides, K., 134n
Korsakov, S. S., 156
Kravkov, 193
Kuleshova, Roza, 156-58
Kuliabko, A. A., 193, 196
kymograph, 104-05

Lafontaine (Swiss magnetizer) 54
Langlois, 33
Language, power of, in hypnosis, 60
Lapitsky, Dr., 155
Laplace (Pierre-Simon), 177

Lateaux, stigmata case of, 83
Lavoisier (Antoine-Laurent), 50, 51
Lazarev, P. P., 116, 136-37, 140, 141
Lehmann, A., 43n, 67n, 104-05, 178
Leningrad, 3, 171n; Admiralty, 109; Institute of the Brain, 171
Léonie B., case of, 33-34
Leontiev, A. N., 158
Leontovich, A. V., 143
Lethargy/lethargics, 37ff, 62, 65
Levenfeld, L., 41, 46
Liébeault, 54, 69
Lifshitz, Yasha, 175-76, 177
Lunatism, *see* Somnabulism

MacDougall, 132
Maeterlinck (Maurice), 190
Mager, Henri, 153
Malpighian tubes, 170, 172
Marey tambour, 113
Marx, Karl, 5, 107n
Materialism, 7, 8, and *passim*
Mayorov, F. P., 27n, 31
Mazepa, 125
Mechanical hand, *see* Hand
Mechnikov, I. I., 43-45
Mediumism, *see* Spiritism
Mendeleev, D. I., 51, 106, 154n, 178, 179n, 204
Mental: broadcasting, *see* Brain broadcasting; suggestion, *see* Suggestion; transmission, *see* Telepathy
Mesmer/mesmerism, 49-52. *See also* Hypnotism
Messing, Wolf/V. G., 111n, 114n
Metallic screening, as factor in transmission of mental suggestion, 142ff
Metapsychology, *see* Parapsychology
Middle Ages, 4, 12, 48, 70
Mikhaylov, F., 31n

"Mind-reading"/"muscle-reading," 72, 111ff
Mitchell, Dr., 154
Mock: burns, 75-76; blows, 75; death, see Death; feeding, 74; fever, 74
Mori, 14
Moscow, 121; Prosthetic and Orthopedic Institute, 109; University of, 195
"Muscle-reading," see "Mind-reading"
Muscular power, transmission of, in space, see Telekinesis
Myers, F. W. H., 7n, 123n

Nantes, 67, 97
Nautilus, 144
Negovsky, V. A., 202-03
Neuromuscular superexcitability, 62-63
Neuropsychic phenomena, 5, 6
Nizhni-Tagil Pedagogic Institute, 156
Nudov, Dr., 13

Odessa, 175
Oks, B., 17-18
Oneiromancy, 12
Ore-divining, see Water- and ore-divining
Orsk, 4
Osis, Karlis, 191-92
Ossovetsky, Stefan, 159-61
Osty, Eugène and Marcel, telekinetic experiments of, 180ff
Ostrovskaya, O. O., 121
Ostrovsky, Nikolay, 121
Ovsyannikov-Kulikovsky, 176
Oxford (University), 195

P. and Z. (students), case of, 86-87
Padua, University of, 195

Pain, insensitivity to, see Insensitivity to pain
Parabiosis/anabiosis, 194ff, 203
Paracelsus, 49
"Paradoxical" phase of sleep, see Sleep
Parapsychology/metapsychology, 6-7, 174, 177, 178, 179, 191, and passim
Paris, 33, 152, 159; Institute for Metapsychology, 180; University of, 50
Pascal (Blaise), 160
Passes, 49-52, 57
Paustovsky, K. G., 175-76
Patriotic War (World War II), 202
Pavlov, I. P., 8, 17, 18, 19, 20, 22-23, 25, 27, 40, 45, 55-56, 57, 58n, 59-60, 63, 79, 89, 134, 158; experiments of, in conditioned reflexes, 22-23; theory of dreams, 23ff; two-signal-systems theory, 23ff, 60, 134
Perepel, I. A., 30
Perikhanyats, Ya. I., 72n, 160-63
Peter I, 195
Petrov, F. P., 141n
Petrovna, Tamara, case of, 4
Petrovsky, A., 139
peyotl, effects of, 70-72, 161
Pilgrim's Frank Story to His Spiritual Father, 96-97
Pilsudsky, 160
Planchette, 132
Platonov, K. I., 74, 134
Podmore, Frank, 51n, 123n, 178
Podyapolsky, P. P., 75-76
Poe, Edgar Allan, 39
Polotsky Psychiatric Hospital, 155
Popov, A. S., 136
Posnikov, Piotr, 195
"Possession," 85
Pravda, 155
Pravdich-Neminsky, Prof., 138n

Preier, 112, 113
Price, George, 179-80
Prince, Walter, 132
Probability theory, 29, 126, 174, 184
Prokop, O., 151n
Psychic epidemics, *see* Epidemics
Puységur, 52-53
Psychogenous illness, 87-88, 91
Psychokinesis, *see* Telekinesis

Rapport, between hypnotist and hypnotic, 58ff, 78-79
Reincarnation, 7-8, 189
Religion, as fostering superstition, 8, 120, 187, 191, and *passim*
Renaissance, the, hypnotism during, 48-49
Reutler, Rudolf, experiments of, on Asiatic locusts, 170-71, 172, 184
Revival, 194ff; of cat, 197ff; of dog, 195; of human beings, 202-03
Rhine, Dr., 127-28, 164, 165, 180; experiments of, with dice, 172-74
Riche, P., 63n
Richet, Charles, 7n, 32, 164; experiments of: with Ossovetsky, 159-61, 164, 165; in guessing playing cards, 152; in telesthesia, with Léonie B., 33-34
Richmond, 172
Ringer-Lock's fluid, 197
Rochas, A. de, 188-89
Rochester (city), 101
Roman Catholic Church, 187
Rome/Romans, 48, 150
Rosenthal, Dr., 38-39
Rosh Pina (Palestine), 170
Rouhier, 70
Roux, J., 7n

Russia/Soviet Union, 5, 55, 112n, 120, 142, and *passim*

"Sabbath flight," 70
St. Petersburg University Physical Society, 204n
Sauerbruch, F., 140
Schiff, 195
Schmidt, 153
Schneider, Rudi, telekinetic experiments with, 180ff
Schumann, W., 140
Sensibilization of skin, 158
Shakhnovich, M., 108n
Schwarzenberg, Princess, 88
Schwenter, 49
Sechenov, I. M., 8, 27, 108
Sense organs, supernormal sharpening of, 154ff, 164
Shilo, Dr., 155
Shor, 193
Siamese twins, experiment with, 19
Signal systems, in brain, *see* Pavlov
Simon, M., 67n, 68, 69-70
Sinclair, Upton and Mary, experiments of, in transmission of drawings, 132ff
Skalovsky, A. N., 126
Sleep, 11ff; autohypnotic, 49-53; and dreams, 8, 11ff; hypnotic, *see* hypnosis; paradoxical phase of, 25; Pavlov's theory of, 23ff, 45, and *passim;* prolonged/lethargic, 37ff; somnabulistic, 42ff; therapy, 21
Sleepwalking, *see* Somnabulism
Soal, Dr., 127, 129
Society of Experimental Psychology, Russian, 112
Society for Psychical Research: American, 189; London, 120, 122-23, 189
Society of Physicists, St. Petersburg University, 106-07

Somnabulism, 42ff, 65, 72-74
Soul, existence of, after death,
  187ff
Soviet Union, see Russia
Spiritism/spiritualism/
  mediumism, 8, 47-48, 101-16,
  165, 176, 177, 178
Split personality, 45-46, 73
Steblin, V. S., experiments of, in
  telekinesis, 171-72, 184
Stigmata, appearance of, 83
Stradonitz, Kekule von, 28
Stylites, 64
Sudre, P., 160
Suggestion, mental/verbal, 6,
  37ff, 44, 50, 53, 83-98,
  115-16, 134, 184, and passim;
  during hypnotic state, 37ff;
  during waking state, 6, 83-98.
  See also Autosuggestion
Superstition(s): associated with
  death, 7, 187-204; and dreams,
  28ff; fostered by mysterious
  phenomena, 3-8; fostered by
  religion, 8, 120, 187
"Sympathetic" remedies, curing
  by, 90-91

Tari, Dr., 37-38
Tarkhanov, I. R., 41-43, 87-88,
  102
Tartini (composer), 28
Tchaikovsky, 125
Telekinesis/psychokinesis, 6,
  149, 169-84, 188
Telepathy/"brain broadcasting,"
  6, 115, 116-45, 149, 162, 164,
  174n, 178, and passim
Telesthesia, 6, 29ff, 149, 174n
Terentiev, P. V., 72, 161-63
Tertullian, 108
Thought transference, see
  Telepathy
Thanatology, 8, 192ff. See also
  Death

Thouless, R. H., experiments of,
  with dice, 174, 180
Tischner, R., experiment of, in
  telesthesia, 130-31
Tolstoy, Leo, 107
Tomsk Institute of Technology,
  151
To-Rama, 93-94
Townsend, Col., 42
Trance, 154; lethargic, 38-39.
  See also Hypnosis;
  Autohypnosis
Transmission/perception,
  unmediated: of muscular
  power, see Telekinesis; of
  thought, see Telepathy; of
  visual objects, see Telesthesia
Triumfov, A. V., 141
Tugarinov, V. P., 145n
Turgenev, I. S., 124-25
Turlygin, S. Ya., 141n, 142
Twain, Mark, 124
"Two Mothers"
  (Ostrovskaya's story), 121
Tyndall, 120

Ukhtomsky, A. A., 76-77, 95, 98
United States/America, 7n,
  101-02, 120, 127, 136, and
  passim
Utrecht, 136

Van Helmont, 49
Volkers (American physicist),
  169n
Volta's pile, 38
Valter, G., 41
Vasiliev, L. L., 72n, 77n, 114n,
  125; experiments of, 113-14,
  144n, 161-63
Victor (patient of Puységur), 52
Voltaire, 28
Vvedensky, N. E., 13, 47, 73, 83,
  84n, 194

Waking state, 17ff; suggestion and autosuggestion during, 83-98. *See also* Excitation; Sleep
Warcollier, R., 7n
Warsaw, 159
Warts, removing of, by hypnosis, 90-91
Water- ore-divining, 150ff, 164
"Wax flexibility" of bodily members, in hypnosis, 63-64
Wells, H., 31n
Weygandt, 14

"Witches' salves," 70
World War I, 93; II, 202n

Yanvareva, I. A., 197, 198n
Yefimov, V. V., 40n, 110
Yelabug, 86
Yogis, trance of, 40-41

Zener's cards, 127-30, 133, 162, 164
Zorab, G., 136n
Zvezda, 155
Zweig, Stefan, 53n